Further Praise

"In *Combating Hatred*, Terrance Furin confronts current and aspiring leaders with the reality that acts of hatred will continue to significantly impact the goals of education. Yet at the same time, Furin draws on a diverse set of thought leaders, from legendary educational thinkers to everyday teachers, to share strategies on how to navigate these challenges in equity-oriented ways. For me, the power of *Combating Hatred* rests in Furin's seamless weaving of historical and contemporary events, transformational leadership theory, and his own wisdom of practice."

—Aimee LaPointe Terosky, EdD, Professor of Educational Leadership, Saint Joseph's University

"The timing of Terrance Furin's latest book cannot be more appropriate. With the recent proliferation of school violence in the form of shootings and the disturbing incidents of hate crimes, along with the insurrection by white supremacists on our nation's Capitol on January 6th, we as a nation are at an existential inflection point in our nation's history. *Combating Hatred for the Soul of America: Watershed Moments for Transformational Educators*, third in the Combating Hatred series, will prove to be a valuable resource for all educators truly interested in finding ways to confront and uproot systemic racism, ensure the safety and welfare of their students, and make a difference in our society. Furin uses the very effective case study method to reveal strategies that can be helpful in building understanding and harmony among all elements of the school community. *Combating Hatred* is an important guidebook for school leaders, as it brings theory and practice together around the vital topic of confronting hatred and systemic racism. In this new edition, Furin shares his insights gleaned from more than fifty years as an extraordinarily effective and creative educational leader."

—Robert Palestini Ed.D, Professor of Educational Leadership Emeritus; Former Dean of Graduate and Continuing Studies; Founding Executive Director of the Educational Leadership Institute and Center for Catholic Urban Education at SJU

Combating Hatred for the Soul of America

Combating Hatred for the Soul of America

Watershed Moments for Transformational Educators

Third Edition

Terrance L. Furin

ROWMAN & LITTLEFIELD
Lanham • Boulder • New York • London

Published by Rowman & Littlefield
An imprint of The Rowman & Littlefield Publishing Group, Inc.
4501 Forbes Boulevard, Suite 200, Lanham, Maryland 20706
www.rowman.com

86-90 Paul Street, London EC2A 4NE, United Kingdom

Copyright © 2022 by Terrance L. Furin

All rights reserved. No part of this book may be reproduced in any form or by any electronic or mechanical means, including information storage and retrieval systems, without written permission from the publisher, except by a reviewer who may quote passages in a review.

British Library Cataloguing in Publication Information Available

Library of Congress Cataloging-in-Publication Data Available

ISBN 9781475865066 (cloth : alk. paper)
ISBN 9781475865073 (pbk. : alk. paper)
ISBN 9781475865080 (ebook)

DEDICATION
For my wife Mary Ann who has given Varykyno and so much more.
For my children, Kathleen, Jennifer, Timothy, and Molly
who are my best teachers.
For my grandchildren,
Jasmine, Aya, Chaundra, Timothy, Saoirse, Santana, and Emiliano.
May they know a world without hatred.

Contents

List of Figures — xi

Preface — xiii

Acknowledgments — xv

Introduction: Watershed Challenges and Opportunities for Transformational Educators — xvii

1 The Power of Symbols: Dixie—a Flag and a Song — 1

2 The Power of Symbols: Hanging Nooses, Institutionalized Racism, and Educators Building Bridges across Racial Divides — 11

3 The Power of Symbols: Auschwitz, Anti-Semitism, and a School Prayer Crisis — 29

4 Combating a Neo-Nazi Hate Group — 45

5 Transformational Educators Combating Student Alienation — 57

6 Transformational Leadership — 81

7 Inspirational Transformational Educational Leaders — 91

8 Becoming Transformational Educational Leaders through Personal Growth — 125

9 Creating Communities of Learners — 139

About the Author — 157

List of Figures

Figure 0.1	U.S. Racism Dialectic	xviii
Figure 2.1	Social Structure of the Antebellum South	19
Figure 4.1	Dialectic and Change Dynamics	52
Figure 5.1	Traditional School District Organizational Chart	59
Figure 5.2	Student at the Center of the Organizational Structure for Education	63
Figure 6.1	Essential Qualities of Mission, Vision, and Community	83
Figure 8.1	Lowney's Four Pillars of Success	126
Figure 8.2	Soul of Our Nation	130
Figure 9.1	The Bluest Eye	145
Figure 9.2	Representation of the Lighthouse	153

Preface

Three powerful emotions caused me to write this book: love, fear, and faith. Let me explain.

- Love

I have a deep love for American history and our core democratic values of equality and social justice for all citizens. I consider these as being the essence of America's soul. This love for our country began with my earliest indelible childhood memories. They are of World War II and the feeling of common unity and purpose which stirred something deep within me.

I can still hear Gabriel Heatter's radio voice giving us the latest news, feel the sense of confusion when blankets were hung over windows during blackouts, grow weary thinking of the long waits in the 1936 Ford as my mother stood in line for hours at the butcher store to buy any rationed meat (if any was available), feel the excitement of playing with friends and writing "Kilroy was here" on slate sidewalks with bits of coal that didn't make it into the furnace, remember having to put two fingers under my nose to represent Hitler's mustache when I was chosen to be the bad guy in the game of "Yanks versus Notsies" (that is how I first spelled Nazis), and so very much more.

This love blossomed when I became a history major in undergraduate school and then taught history and government to junior and senior high school students for twelve years. At this same time, I went to graduate school and received my master's degree in history and later my PhD in American Studies from Case Western Reserve University in Cleveland.

Even though my love of country is deep-seated, I have a love for something that exceeds it. This is a deep sense of spirituality founded on the basic belief that every life is sacred. The Jesuit principle of *cura personalis* (care of the person) strongly resonates with me. This is one of the main reasons that I wrote this book.

- Fear

I have a dreadful fear that two of our core national values—equality and social justice for all citizens—are under attack and that our very soul as a nation is in danger of extinction. This fear gripped me as I, as well as millions of other Americans, watched mobs of rioters attack our nation's Capitol on January 6.

I felt that I must do something to protect and help advance our core values. As luck would have it for me, Tom Koerner from Rowman & Littlefield emailed me to see if I might be interested in writing another edition of the *Combating Hatred* series. I readily agreed because I have faith that our democracy can survive if we stand up for our democratic principles.

- Faith

A key to my belief that we can preserve our democracy is found in witnessing the power inherent in all educators. We have opportunities every day to make meaningful differences not only in the lives of our students but of entire communities as well. As a school superintendent for twenty-two years I have seen this power manifested in numerous examples as educators became true transformational leaders—leaders who realized their own agency and began to create a future based upon our core values.

This book is really about them. They hold our future in their hands. The challenges are great—but so are the rewards. Our very survival as a democratic nation depends on them—and upon you.

TLF

Acknowledgments

Acknowledgments need to be given to the editors of publications for granting permission to reprint portions of material that appeared elsewhere. Reprinted with permission from *School Administrator* magazine, published by AASA, the school superintendents association, are the following: the February 2004 issue of *School Administrator* for "Tragedy at the Top" by Terrance L. Furin; the November 2007 issue of *School Administrator* for "Confronting a Neo-Nazi Hate Group" by Terrance L. Furin; and the November 2017 issue of *School Administrator* for "Combating Hatred Among Us" by Terrance L. Furin.

An earlier version of the "Motorhead Club" contained in chapter 5 appeared in an article titled "Cult of Self: Arrogance and the Death of History" in *Culture Clash/Media Demons*, copyright 2004 by Chelsea House Publishers and an imprint of Infobase Learning.

An earlier version describing *Fe y Algeria* in Bolivia appeared in the Jesuit journal *Conversations* (Furin, Terrance L. (2005) "A 'House of Learning' High in the Andes," *Conversations on Jesuit Higher Education*, Vol. 27, Article 8).

Acknowledgment is also given to Mike Wall for using his unpublished poem, "Inishmore," which is included in a case study of him.

I wish to acknowledge the many wonderful professionals who gave of their time to read portions of the manuscript before it became a book and who provided endorsements: Jay Goldman, editor of AASA's *School Administrator*; Harris Sokoloff, University of Pennsylvania; Connie Kindler, Pennsylvania Association of School Administrators; and Aimee Tersoky and Robert Palestini, Saint Joseph's University.

Special thanks also go to the individuals who are presented as case studies in this book as they have read the section that concerns them and, in some cases, other portions of the book: they are Mike Wall, Tiara Grymes, Frank

Murphy, Ellen Keys, Marty Kane, Tom Asad, David Jarvie, Sister Rosemary Hocevar, Jack Thomas, and Lucille Lang, the wife of Leonard Lang who is deceased.

Very special thanks go to my wife, Mary Ann, who is a voracious reader and a student of the English language. She has provided invaluable insight on an ongoing basis.

Acknowledgments are also given the professionalism of my editors Tom Koerner, Kira Hall, and Carlie Wall at Rowman & Littlefield who have treated me with the utmost respect and provided valuable editing and publishing suggestions. Without them, especially Tom Koerner, this book would have never been written.

Introduction

Watershed Challenges and Opportunities for Transformational Educators

Let's begin by saying that we are living through a very dangerous time. Everyone in this room is in one way or another aware of that. We are in a revolutionary situation, no matter how unpopular that word has become in this country. The society in which we live is desperately menaced, not by Khrushchev, but from within.[1]

America is not the world and if America is going to become a nation, she must find a way—and this child must help her to find a way to use the tremendous potential and tremendous energy which this child represents. If this country does not find a way to use that energy, it will be destroyed by that energy.[2]

—James Baldwin

WATERSHED CHALLENGES AND OPPORTUNITIES

The two quotations cited above are from James Baldwin's speech, "A Talk to Teachers," delivered in New York City on October 16, 1963. The first quotation is the beginning of his speech in which he focused on the challenges that many of America's Black children faced in the 1960s. The second quotation ends the speech and is the climax of his advice to teachers regarding the rich education needed for Black children to find their identity as well as their sense of agency so as to realize their dreams as American citizens.

The timing of Baldwin's speech followed the tragic Sunday school bombing of a Black church in Birmingham, Alabama, on September 15, 1963. Four young Black girls were killed and many others injured. This became one of the catalysts—and a watershed moment—that led to the Civil Rights Act of

1964 and the Voting Rights Act of 1965. Sixty years later, we find ourselves in a similar watershed moment.

Ours is a time of a profound human relations' crisis wherein our professed national values—especially equality and justice for all—are often out of sync with realities. Vicious hate-filled conflicts are fueled by some of the 838 hate groups[3] which the Southern Poverty Law Center (SPLC) has identified across the United States.[4] As an example, in Pennsylvania alone, there are thirty-six identified groups such as the Loyal Knights of the Ku Klux Klan, the Revolutionary Black Panther Party, and the Blood and Honour Social Club.[5]

Hate-filled conflicts are dominated by, but are not limited to, White-Black/Black-White racism. There are also violent clashes involving Jewish, Asian, Muslim, Native American, and other minority groups. A race relations dialectic—buzzing with social, political, and judicial tensions—can be pictured something like this (figure 0.1).

For educators, especially those hoping to be transformational leaders, the challenges are enormous; so are the opportunities. Here is a chance to make real, fundamental changes in relationships that define our culture and our nation's soul. That is what this book is about—laying out real-life situations and providing examples of transformational educators combating hatred on the frontlines.

This book builds upon two previous editions in the *Combating Hatred* series.[6] Several accounts of educators combating hatred contained in those editions are in the current book as well. There are also many new ones. This

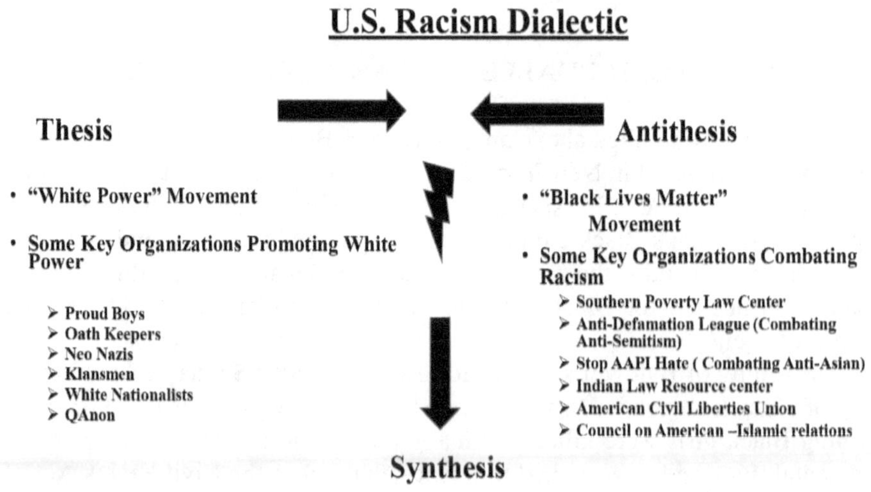

U.S. Racism Dialectic

Thesis

- "White Power" Movement
- Some Key Organizations Promoting White Power
  - Proud Boys
  - Oath Keepers
  - Neo Nazis
  - Klansmen
  - White Nationalists
  - QAnon

Antithesis

- "Black Lives Matter" Movement
- Some Key Organizations Combating Racism
  - Southern Poverty Law Center
  - Anti-Defamation League (Combating Anti-Semitism)
  - Stop AAPI Hate (Combating Anti-Asian)
  - Indian Law Resource center
  - American Civil Liberties Union
  - Council on American –Islamic relations

Synthesis

Figure 0.1 U.S. Racism Dialectic.

author is personally familiar with all of the examples and knows the individuals detailed in them.

One of the reasons for this new edition is the fact that the hatred temperature has risen significantly since the second edition was published in 2019. In fact, that temperature—fueled by the death of George Floyd and the subsequent Black Lives Matter movement coupled with the riot at the nation's Capitol on January 6—has gone beyond the boiling point. It has melted social constructs and created malleable opportunities for substantive change.

EDUCATORS COMBATING HATRED

The center of the "Racism Dialectic" can be an extremely uncomfortable hot zone. If, however, you are seeking to be an educator who wants to make a real difference, this is the place to be. It is a place where schools and communities can become transformed. It is a place where core American values such as "life, liberty, and the pursuit of happiness"[7] can be more fully realized for all of our citizens. This book explores real-life examples of educators creating opportunities to combat hatred in challenging times.

Here is an overview of the book's nine chapters.

CHAPTER 1, "THE POWER OF SYMBOLS: DIXIE—A FLAG AND A SONG"

The January 6, 2021, riot was the first time that the Confederate flag, a symbol of Dixie, was inside the Capitol building. Another symbol of Dixie is the song itself. When it was played by the band at a high school football game to celebrate a touchdown for the home team, it caused a Black teacher at the school to protest as he and his girlfriend were offended by the playing of a song that celebrates both treason and slavery. This chapter details the ways that the school district's superintendent encountered this act.

Here is a summary of the chapter:

- Symbols can evoke fond or hurtful institutional memories.
- Transformational educators need to be sensitive to the rights of all individuals.
- Educators need to be aware of symbols and other signs that are hurtful to some members of a diverse population.
- Teachable moments often require interdisciplinary strategies to move beyond entrenched positions.

- Transparent communications with multiple individuals and publics are the fuel for successful teachable moments that can become the lifeblood of a democratic society.

CHAPTER 2, "THE POWER OF SYMBOLS: HANGING NOOSES, INSTITUTIONALIZED RACISM, AND EDUCATORS BUILDING BRIDGES ACROSS RACIAL DIVIDES"

One of the most vivid images of the January 6 riot at the Capitol is that of a noose hanging from a large, newly constructed wooden beam. This chapter details the racial hatred inherent in the image—and reality—of hanging noses.

This chapter considers ways that:

- the symbol of hanging nooses is indicative of institutionalized racism;
- the masks that people wear often hide true beliefs regarding racial values;
- the failure of Reconstruction led to the continuation of the economic, political, and social structure of the Ante-Bellum South and raises the question as to who won the Civil War;
- the strength of the Black Codes and Jim Crow laws continued institutionalized racism and provides the basis for radical White supremacist groups today;
- educators built bridges across racial divides.

CHAPTER 3, "THE POWER OF SYMBOLS: AUSCHWITZ, ANTI-SEMITISM, AND A SCHOOL PRAYER CRISIS"

This chapter details ways that a school superintendent combated anti-Semitism and community uproar when the school valedictorian, a young Jewish woman, initiated a federal restraining order against Christian prayer at the graduation ceremony.

Here is an outline of the chapter:

- A knowledge of history, particularly regarding human rights and social justice for all members of our society, is essential in combating hatred.
- Hatred is often based upon a herd mentality.
- A strong sense of personal agency is essential to combating hatred.
- Interdisciplinary approaches can turn potentially hostile confrontations into opportunities for creating deep and productive dialogue.

CHAPTER 4, "COMBATING A NEO-NAZI HATE GROUP"

This chapter presents a school district crisis that occurred when a group of neo-Nazis circulated a recruitment flyer which called for a school-wide boycott to honor Heinrich Himmler (head of the dreaded Nazi SS troops). Led by high school teachers, the community came together and formed several unity coalitions to combat this form of hatred.

This chapter encourages educators to:

- be aware of hate groups that may be operating in their area;
- take all threats seriously;
- have clear policies in place that deal with hate groups and threats to schools;
- communicate clearly, completely, and often regarding hate groups and threats to school safety;
- utilize various state and national resources and organizations that have experience in dealing with hate groups;
- understand the dynamics of change and aim to institutionalize positive changes that come from teachable moments created by hate-filled crises.

CHAPTER 5, "TRANSFORMATIONAL EDUCATORS COMBATING STUDENT ALIENATION"

This chapter explores the roots of student alienation that often lead to hatred and violent eruptions. It presents some possible philosophical and theoretical explanations that are often found in the structure of schooling itself. Several examples of educators who moved outside of the established norm to create educational experiences that honor and nourish all students are presented.

This chapter:

- considers the role that high-stakes testing can have in leading to student alienation and the potential for violence;
- presents a child-centered philosophy that recognizes the inherent importance of each student;
- presents examples of teachers whose strong sense of agency and creativity provided experiences that nourished all students.

CHAPTER 6, "TRANSFORMATIONAL LEADERSHIP"

This chapter presents a definition of transformational leadership as differentiated from transactional leadership—a distinction provided by James

MacGregor Burns in his book *Transforming Leadership*. It develops three key components of transformational leadership as follows:

- mission,
- vision, and
- community.

The union of the three creates a powerful force that enables leaders to become transformational. Each of these components is developed in depth with practical examples that combine theory and practice.

CHAPTER 7, "INSPIRATIONAL TRANSFORMATIONAL EDUCATIONAL LEADERS"

This chapter presents eight different transformational educational leaders. These examples are not nationally well-known "stars" but rather educators whose day-to-day activities on the frontlines of educational change contain important lessons for educators everywhere. This author has been inspired by all of them and has worked alongside many of them as they became transformational and combated hatred in their own unique ways.

CHAPTER 8, "BECOMING TRANSFORMATIONAL LEADERS THROUGH PERSONAL GROWTH"

Personal growth is a powerful key to becoming a transformational leader and combating hatred. One of the prominent failures among educators and students, in general, is the lack of in-depth knowledge of our nation's core values and history. This can lead to a lack of understanding which often results in prejudice and hatred.

Here is an outline of this chapter:

- leadership, especially transformational leadership, springs from within.
- four pillars of success that enabled the Jesuits to survive for more than 460 years are self-awareness, ingenuity, love, and heroism.
- the "Y" tagline of mind, spirit, and body is a reminder that personal meditation needs to be included with daily physical exercise and intellectual activity.
- regular meditation on America's common core values is necessary to be a transformational leader within our democracy.
- five touchstones are keys to being an effective transformational leader who is knowledgeable regarding America's common core values. These touchstones

are the Declaration of Independence; the United States Constitution and Bill of Rights; the 13th, 14th, 15th, and 19th Amendments to the United States Constitution; *Brown v. Board of Education* Supreme Court Decision; and the Civil Rights Act of 1964 and the Voting Rights Act of 1965.

CHAPTER 9, "CREATING COMMUNITIES OF LEARNERS"

This chapter begins and ends with a quotation from Maxine Greene that challenges us to build communities of learners that imagine alternatives for what our lives and the lives of the group could become. From this opening quotation we explore:

- some ways to create professional learning communities through aesthetic experiences for both teachers and students;
- examples of bonding through professional books to create professional learning communities;
- examples of bonding through award-winning literature;
- ways to build a sense of community through knowledge of our nation's core values.

Following these considerations of professional learning communities, the chapter presents the concept of public pedagogy as specifically seen in the chaos created over critical race theory (CRT). These reactions describe:

- a concept of authentic dialogue;
- a strategic-planning process;
- specific ways to develop a school district's mission and embodiment of it in a mission statement;
- several strategies for transformational educational leaders to build bridges so as to communicate effectively with several different constituencies across a school district.

Chapter 1, "The Power of Symbols: Dixie—a Flag and a Song," takes us to the center of the racism dialectic. Let us learn more about ways that a school superintendent confronted the playing of *Dixie* at a high school football game.

NOTES

1. "A Talk to Teachers" By James Baldwin (Delivered October 16, 1963, as "The Negro Child—His Self-Image" was originally published in The Saturday Review,

December 21, 1963, and reprinted in The Price of the Ticket, Collected Non-Fiction 1948–1985, Saint Martins, 1985.), https://www.spps.org/cms/lib010/MN01910242/Centricity/Domain/125/baldwin_atalktoteachers_1_2.pdf (accessed, July 23, 2021).

2. Ibid.

3. Southern Poverty Law Center definition of a hate group, https://www.splcenter.org/20200318/frequently-asked-questions-about-hate-groups#hate%20group (accessed July 22, 2021). The SPLC defines a hate group as "an organization or collection of individuals that—based on its official statements or principles, the statements of its leaders, or its activities—has beliefs or practices that attack or malign an entire class of people."

4. Hate Map, Southern Poverty Law Center, https://www.splcenter.org/hate-map (accessed July 22, 2021).

5. In 2020 36 Hate Groups Were Tracked in Pennsylvania, https://www.splcenter.org/states/pennsylvania (accessed July 22, 2021).

6. The first is *Combating Hatred: Educators Leading the Way*, Rowman & Littlefield, 2009 and the second is *Combating Hatred: Transformational Educators Striving for Social Justice*, Rowman & Littlefield, 2019.

7. Declaration of Independence, a transcription, https://www.archives.gov/founding-docs/declaration-transcript (accessed July 25, 2021).

Chapter 1

The Power of Symbols
Dixie—a Flag and a Song

I wish I was in the land of cotton,
   Old times there are not forgotten;
   Look away! Look away! Look away! Dixie Land.
   In Dixie's Land where I was born in,
   Early on one frosty morning,
   Look away! Look away! Look away! Dixie Land.[1]

CONFEDERATE FLAG IN STATUARY HALL

On January 6, 2021, a Confederate flag was marched through the Capitol's Statuary Hall for the first time. The blue crossbars containing thirteen white stars on a bright red background represent the slave states of the Confederacy. It is more than a piece of fabric. Today it is a racist symbol that evokes the Civil War Confederacy, indeed an entire civilization, based upon slavery. It symbolizes both the heroic Lost Cause reminiscent of Ante-Bellum times and strong Post-Bellum hatred based on the desire to segregate the White and Black races.

Consider three examples from the movies of sentimental Ante-Bellum images:

- Shirley Temple sweetly receiving birthday gifts from plantation slave children before tapping rhythms while Bojangles dances to the delight of her birthday guests as depicted in *The Littlest Rebel* (1935).
- Idyllic images of Margaret Mitchell's Scarlett O'Hara being primped by Mammy before joyfully riding off to a picturesque barbeque at Twelve Oaks before her civilization was *Gone with the Wind* (1940).

- Joel Chandler Harris's Uncle Remus tales featured in Disney's *Song of the South* (1946) wherein Uncle Remus tenderly sings "Zip-a-Dee-Doo-Dah" where "everything is 'satisfactch'll".[2]

The flag also embodies a hate-filled philosophy's manifestations as seen in these three examples:

- Confederate Vice President Alexander Stephens's Cornerstone speech wherein speaking about the new Confederate government he proclaimed "its foundations are laid, its corner-stone rests, upon the great truth that the negro is not equal to the white man; that slavery subordination to the superior race is his natural and normal condition";[3]
- Little Rock Central High School's desegregation (September 4, 1957) when nine students endured hate-filled racial slurs and threats as they were barred from entering the school until President Eisenhower ordered federal troops to protect them;
- The "Bloody Sunday" march (March 7, 1965) across the Edmund Pettus bridge when 600 people demonstrating for Blacks' voting rights were clubbed and beaten as they attempted to make their way from Selma to Montgomery, Alabama.

These six descriptions provide a brief, though incomplete, context that may help deconstruct the image flashed across the world of the Confederate flag being paraded through the halls of our nation's Capitol. Another image can help broaden this context.

One of the most emotionally gripping scenes in movie history is that of the Atlanta train-yard filled with hundreds of wounded Confederates from *Gone with the Wind*. Scarlett is searching for Dr. Meade to help deliver Melanie's baby. Caught in shocking confusion, she wanders in and out of agonized soldiers. As the camera pulls away to a panorama of suffering, a rumpled Confederate flag waves in the foreground. Adding to the image of defeat and pathos is the music—a blend of Stephen Foster's "Swanee River" with the favored song of the South—"Dixie."

"Dixie"

Daniel Decauter Emmett was a Northerner whose song "Dixie" was popular in both the North and the South after being first performed by Bryant's Minstrels (blackface) in New York City on April 4, 1859. Although it was popular in the North—even Lincoln was reported to like the tune—it quickly became adopted by Confederate army bands and spread throughout the South as a type of Southern anthem.

The foot-tapping tune remains popular today and, similar to the Confederate flag, still evokes images of the idealized Ante-Bellum South. Because of its ties to the slave society, it is seen by many as a symbol of deep-seated racism. This association between the song and racism is repugnant to many, among them the country band "The Dixie Chicks." The BBC reported on June 25, 2020, that the band dropped "Dixie" from their name.

The song had the same reaction regarding racism at a local high school when it was played by the band after the team scored a touchdown. Offended by this, a Black high school teacher, who was at the game with his date, protested the playing of the song. It became a major controversy in the district that eventually landed in the superintendent's lap.

"Dixie" at a High School Football Game: Teachable Moments

A Friday night high school football game often captures a slice of America that dreams are made of: the crispness of an early autumn evening, the sun exiting in the western sky; a grandstand buzzing with young and old, parents and students, community boosters—all anticipating the start of the fall ritual; cheerleaders in their red and white uniforms skipping, twirling, and attempting to unite the buzz of the crowd; sounds of the band playing in-and-out of tune, preparing to trumpet the Wildcats entrance onto the green, brightly lit field. There is a warm sense of community, a glow radiating into the night. Indeed a nice place to be.

This was the setting in the Owen J. Roberts school district located in suburban/rural Philadelphia on a Friday night in 1998. The school district and high school are named after Owen J. Roberts, a conservative 1930s Supreme Court Justice who resided on a 700 acre farm located in the district.

On this Friday night, the high school enrolled approximately 1,200 students of whom 95 percent were White. The school complex with its array of athletic fields shares space with the middle school atop a hillside surrounded by the rolling beginnings of the Appalachians. The school district is a peaceful place dotted with horse farms and stone buildings dating to the 1700s. This is a place to live gently; a place for children to grow into adulthood away from the turmoil of the big city; a place apart from conflicts associated with racism.

For some, on a particular Friday night in 1998, the warm sense of community began to change. Racism was not isolated to the big city. It was on display in Owen J. Roberts when the band spontaneously began to play "Dixie" after the Wildcats scored a touchdown. A Black high school teacher and his girlfriend were at the game. They suddenly felt isolated—and offended. They knew that "Dixie" as well as the Confederate flag are often associated with racial segregation and unequal civil rights. They felt no longer a part of this community and left the stadium. In all probability, they were unnoticed by anyone else in the crowd.

The Monday following the game the teacher told the principal that they had been personally offended. They were also concerned that many Black students may have been offended but were afraid to speak up. The principal assured them that the song would not be played again and that he would begin an investigation into the matter. This situation has a sad ending for the teacher involved—indeed, an even sadder one for the school district. The teacher left the district at the end of the year in part because of the "Dixie" incident. He also had been hurt by repeated racist comments made (under the breath, so to speak) by some faculty members.

After the "Dixie" episode, the principal met with the band director and learned that the song was not officially part of the band's repertoire but that parts of it were spontaneously played by some band members after a hometown touchdown was scored. The principal told the director to stop this practice. When the director told the students of this decision, some were upset and said that they felt their civil liberties, specifically their First Amendment rights, were being violated. They also told him that they planned to do something about his decision.

This was not an idle threat. The band in this community had a very active booster organization. The self-designated student leader of the group who played "Dixie" was the son of the school board president. Here was a bright member of the junior class whose leadership was recognized beyond the band. It was obvious to the principal that the situation was serious. These factors eventually landed "Dixie" in the superintendent's lap.

After discussing the matter with the high school principal and the band director, the superintendent contacted the teacher and assured him that the matter would be investigated and that the song would no longer be played at football games. The next step was to arrange a meeting with the student, who will be called Jerry, to discuss the situation.

Jerry came to the meeting well-prepared and with a trace of arrogance. He had researched "Dixie" and learned that it was popular in both the North and the South before and during the Civil War. He emphasized that Abraham Lincoln was fond of it and had it played by military bands at the conclusion of the war.

Jerry could not understand how the song was offensive to anyone and indicated that it had been played at several games with no previous complaints. He stressed that he represented several students who felt their Constitutional rights were being violated. After the superintendent thanked him for his research and interest in the matter, a date was set for another meeting to continue the conversation.

It was troubling that this student, a bright young man who obviously possessed leadership potential, was either ignorant of civil rights history or insensitive to the fact that this song could be offensive to some members of the Black community. Either conclusion was a condemnation of an educational system that was supposedly preparing future citizens for their participation in a democracy whose strength was built upon the recognition of minority as well as majority rights. The situation presented an opportunity for educating not only this young man but other students and adults who were following this confrontation closely.

It was obvious from the meeting as well as conversations with the principal and the band director that Jerry was entrenched in his views. This intransigence was strengthened by the support of his peers. Clearly, a persistent discussion of the White/Black racial issue would result in a back-and-forth argument that would not help Jerry or his supporters become more aware of the social justice issues involved.

Because of Jerry's stubbornness on the issue of Black/White racism, the superintendent chose a less-known topic that contained a similar human rights theme for future discussions. This was a segment of history regarding the treatment of minority Native Americans by the dominant White culture.

A Book on Native America Racism—Education for Extinction

At the next meeting, Jerry was given a book to read regarding one aspect of Native American treatment by Whites. It was David Wallace Adams's *Education for Extinction*[4] which is a history of the Native American boarding school experience from 1875 to 1928. This powerful book describes a tragically sad chapter in American history. Many young Native Americans were taken from their families and tribes. They were relocated to boarding schools hundreds or thousands of miles from their homes. One of these was in Carlisle, Pennsylvania, little more than one and one-half hours from the Owen J. Roberts school district.

The main reason for this relocation was that reservation schools, often run by well-intentioned Christian organizations, were not as successful as they might have been. Students would often miss days or weeks at a time, speak in their native languages, and refuse to abandon their cultural traditions. The boarding school concept solved those problems. It stripped Native American students physically, mentally, and spiritually until they were completely naked. They were totally isolated from their families and friends on the reservations.

Their names were changed, often into those of past U.S. presidents or historical figures such as Julius Caesar. They were forbidden to speak their native languages, dress in their customary clothing, discuss their religious beliefs, or mention anything about their cultural traditions. They could speak only English, wore military-style uniforms, listened for hours to sermons about Christianity, and were forced to learn Christian songs and prayers.

Violations of the numerous rules often meant brushing their teeth with strong lye, enduring severe whippings, marching for hours, and suffering other cruel forms of corporal and mental punishment.

Once stripped of their identities, they were reconstructed in the desired image to be assimilated into the White culture. They learned to eat with knives, forks, and spoons. Males were taught farming skills and trades such as carpentry, tinsmithing, and shoemaking. Females spent their time learning proper Victorian skills for women such as sewing, cleaning, ironing, canning, and cooking.

Photos catch the images of transformation. Two particularly potent ones are found on the back of Adams's book. They are provided by the National Anthropological Archives of the Smithsonian Institution and tell the story of a renamed Navajo, Tom Torlino. The photos were taken three years apart. The before picture is of a noble-looking native with long-flowing hair, earrings, a decorative necklace, and traditional Navajo clothing. The after picture is of a groomed young man with short combed hair dressed in a white shirt, tie, and formal jacket.

These contrasting photos show the outward effects of the boarding school program. What they do not capture is the loneliness, heartache, and despair that accompanied many of the transmutations. Adams describes the human tragedies that this program had on both Native American students and their families. He captures the tears, despair, and eventual emptiness endured by many of these natives. At these schools, compassionate treatment was not the goal. Assimilation was.[5]

Hopefully, Adams's dramatic account of these boarding schools would have an impact on Jerry who was defending "Dixie" as an innocent tune. The superintendent planned for the next meeting to be a discussion about the book. It would also be about more than that. It would be about "Chief Wahoo."

Chief Wahoo

A three-story red and white rendition of "Chief Wahoo" stood atop the main entrance of the Cleveland Indians home at Municipal Stadium on the shores of Lake Erie for more than forty years until the Indians moved to a new home in 1994. The sign is currently in the Crawford Auto and Aviation Museum of the Western Reserve Historical Society. While at the Stadium, it was set on a large pivot so that it could slowly rotate showing all angles of the team's chosen mascot.

Angles, indeed. The bright red mascot head, approximately one-third the size of the entire body, is a series of angles—triangular eyes, pointed eyebrows, hooked nose, broad angular grin, sharp chin, and slanted ears. All of this is topped off with a peaked feather.

Cleveland was one of the founding teams of the American League and began using the mascot name "Indians" in 1915. The Wahoo logo was adopted shortly after World War II and remained in prominent use until 2019 when the team dropped it. Many Clevelanders were embarrassed, especially during a pennant or World Series chase, when widespread media attention sent Wahoo grinning around the world. Nonetheless, passion for the Chief had been strong over the years.

An event in 1998 revealed the depth of that passion. It occurred at an annual conference of United Methodists that was held in Cleveland at which a resolution was introduced urging the members of the church to stop wearing clothing or hats displaying the logo. One woman was quoted by Cleveland's daily newspaper, the *Plain Dealer*, as saying "I would cease being a United Methodist before I would cease wearing my Chief Wahoo clothing."[6] With this in mind, let us return for a third meeting between Jerry and the school superintendent.

At this meeting, Jerry was given a baseball cap featuring the grinning "Wahoo." When asked how he felt about the logo, he admitted that it looked rather silly. He was also given a copy of an editorial cartoon by the famous *Philadelphia Inquirer* editorial cartoonist, Tony Auth.

The cartoon is from October 22, 1997, and is entitled *Can You Imagine?* It contains a drawing of "Chief Wahoo" with the words "The Cleveland INDIANS." Next to this is a rendition of a smiling Asian labeled "The Cleveland ASIANS." Two other drawings and labels complete the cartoon—a grinning African with the words "The Cleveland AFRICANS," and a beaming Hispanic in a sombrero labeled "The Cleveland HISPANICS."

This cartoon had a noticeable impact on Jerry who agreed that the Asian, African, and Hispanic logos would be offensive and should not be used by a major league team. He was still a little undecided about the Indians but was beginning to see that it may also be offensive. Jerry did admit that the Native American boarding schools were an ugly chapter in American history.

When asked if he would wear the baseball cap he said that to wear it in the presence of Native Americans would probably be offensive to them. To wear it in front of others could be offensive only if they were politically correct individuals. To wear it alone in the woods would not offend anyone. But what would this say about his true feelings? No easy answer.

Jerry saw the social justice principle contained in the "Chief Wahoo" example. He began to apply it to the playing of "Dixie." He agreed that it was possible for those who may have experienced racial discrimination and whose ancestors may have suffered from more than 400 years of slavery and the Jim Crow Black Codes to be offended by the song. The meeting ended, and for all practical purposes the matter was closed. Perhaps Jerry's understanding of prejudice and feelings of tolerance grew. Perhaps the various meetings and conversations simply wore him down. In any event, it was a teachable moment for the superintendent, for Jerry, and for his supporters.

One more step was necessary. The superintendent felt a responsibility to share some aspects of this learning experience with teachers, students, and the greater community. An article was written for the district website entitled "Chief Wahoo," or "Should I Wear My Hat," or "Dixie Revisited," "(you choose)." The superintendent began this way.

> One of the treats in growing up in Cleveland following World War II was a continuation of the great feeling of unity that was part of the all-out war effort. It was manifested in many ways—not least of which was the annual struggle among the "boys of summer" for the all-important pennant—the right to represent your league in the World Series. "Chief Wahoo" was the logo for our Cleveland Indians, and he was as much a part positive boyhood memories as the first time [driving] the John Deer[e] tractor or the smell of grandmother's gingerbread cookies.

The article continues by describing some of the impacts that Adams's book had on ways of viewing Native Americans. Auth's cartoon was explained, and it was stated that "'Dixie' carried a lot of baggage about slavery and about being unequal and about being an unrespected member of our society." But "didn't they [the band] have the freedom to play what they desired?"

The article answered the question.

> Alone in the forest, yes. With those who do not object? Maybe. Around those who take offense? No. Our individual rights as citizens of a democracy are limited when they run into the rights of others. The community, the commonwealth, should preserve the integrity and wholeness of each individual for the general good. Sensitivity is a necessity for continued growth, Growth is a necessity for a dynamic democracy.

The article was distributed to teachers and board members and published on the school district's website. Reactions were mostly positive. It is interesting to note that some progress concerning greater sensitivity regarding American multiculturalism has been made. The Chief "Wahoo" logo was dropped by the Cleveland Indians beginning with the 2019 season. The Indians name was changed beginning in 2022. They are now known as the Cleveland Guardians. It was supposedly inspired by the large statues on the pylons for Cleveland's Hope Memorial bridge.

The "Dixie" case study presents one example of ways to combat racial hatred by viewing it as a teaching/learning opportunity. The band's playing "Dixie" and the complaint of a Black faculty member presented special teachable moments. These were openings to educate students, teachers, and the general public. This is an example of reacting to a crisis that ended with positive results. There are times, such as this example, when it is necessary to be reactive. In situations concerning social justice issues, it is far better to be proactive rather than reactive.

To be proactive places a special responsibility on all educational leaders. It demands deep and continuous personal inner reflection relative to racism and social justice issues. It mandates the development of a curriculum and a school environment that is rich in its consideration of multicultural perspectives. Only through carefully planned educational programs can progress be made in combating the ignorance that often surrounds human rights issues and leads to hatred.

SUMMARY: LESSONS LEARNED

- Symbols can evoke fond or hurtful institutional memories. The confederate flag and the song "Dixie" do both. If you are a Southern White, such memories are often very different than if you were Black whose heritage was built on slavery.
- Transformational educators need to be sensitive to the rights of all individuals for whom they are responsible for leading. Such sensitivity comes from continuous reflection and questioning of their inner selves.
- Teachable moments can arise at any time and come from multiple directions. All educators need to be aware of symbols and other signs that are hurtful to some members of a diverse population.
- Teachable moments often require interdisciplinary strategies to move beyond entrenched positions.
- Continuous, transparent communications with multiple individuals and publics are the fuel for successful teachable moments that can become the lifeblood of a democratic society.

The next chapter, "The Power of Symbols: Hanging Nooses, Institutionalized Racism, and Educators Building Bridges across Racial Divides," considers the powerful racist symbol that hanging nooses represents. It also considers the hidden racism that occurred in a school district when a series of explicit racist texts between the superintendent and the athletic director were publicly exposed. The chapter also presents a historical perspective of institutionalized racism. Let us continue to explore the power of symbols from the January 6 riot with the image of a Hanging noose amid chants of "Hang Mike Pence."

NOTES

1. Lyrics to *Dixie* Song, https://haysfreepress.com/2015/07/10/lyrics-to-dixie-song/ (accessed August 1, 2021).

2. Lyrics Zip-a-Dee-Doo-Dah, https://www.google.com/search?q=lrics+zip+a+dee+do+doh&oq=lrics+zip+a+dee+do+doh&aqs=chrome.69i57j0i13j0i8i13i30l8.17063j0j15&sourceid=chrome&ie=UTF-8 (accessed July 31, 2021).

3. Alexander H. Stephens Cornerstone Speech, https://www.battlefields.org/learn/primary-sources/cornerstone-speech (accessed July 31, 2021).

4. David Wallace Adams, *Education for Extinction* (Lawrence, Kansas: University Press of Kansas, 1995).

5. It is interesting to note that after years of fighting to get children's remains returned from the Carlisle, Pennsylvania, boarding school, the Rosebud Sioux were successful in accomplishing this as reported in *The Philadelphia Inquirer* of July 30, 2021.The remains of nine children were returned to the Sioux reservation in South Dakota for a spiritually poignant ceremony and reburial.

6. Karen Long, "Methodists crush bid to oust Wahoo," *Plain Dealer*, June 19, 1998.

Chapter 2

The Power of Symbols

Hanging Nooses, Institutionalized Racism, and Educators Building Bridges across Racial Divides

Capitol mob built gallows and chanted "Hang Mike Pence"[1]
—Washington, DC, 2021

"Incident more hype than reality, Hangman's nooses cause stir in Jena area."[2]
—Jenna, Louisiana, 2006

"Good hangings there!"[3]
—Coatesville, Pennsylvania, 2013

These three examples referring to gallows, nooses, and hangings demonstrate the dreaded power associated with lynchings in the United States. The first quotation concerns the infamous January 6, 2021, Capitol riot where an image captured by Andrew Caballero-Reynolds (AFP/Getty Images) has gallows with a red noose hanging from a brown crossbeam.[4] The photo frames the majestic Capitol building, a symbol of America's faith in democracy, serenely stable under a cloudy blue sky on a cold January day. The contrast between this symbol and the hatred inherent in the hanging noose should strike fear deep into America's soul. The noose poses a threat to the very survival of our democracy's core values.

The second quotation concerns an incident that occurred at a high school in Jena, Louisiana, when some students at a predominantly White high school hung a noose from a tree to intimidate Black students. This was done to keep them from sitting under the only available shade tree during free periods. The investigation that followed revealed attempts to downplay the incident which eventually became a national rallying point for civil rights action.

The third quotation is taken from a series of racial texts that were exchanged between a school district superintendent and the district's athletic director. The texts were eventually made public and led to a crisis in the district as they exposed the true racial beliefs of supposedly trusted school leaders. This crisis uncovered the deep racism that is often hidden by outward masks. The later of these two hate crises took place in schools and should concern all educators.

RACISM AND HANGING NOOSES AT JENA, LOUISIANA, HIGH SCHOOL

The story accompanying the *Jena Times* headline—"Incident more hype than reality, Hangman's nooses cause stir in Jena area"—began when two nooses were found hanging from a large oak tree at Jena High School. The tree provided the only shade in the schoolyard. The *Jena Times* called the event an ignorant prank. The school, located in Louisiana's LaSalle Parish, had approximately 535 students of whom 85 percent were White. The nooses apparently were hung in response to a Black student's question at an assembly as to whether Blacks could also sit under the tree—a space traditionally occupied by Whites only.

The story indicates that the nooses were quietly removed before most students saw them. It also stated that the pranksters were identified and removed from school with a recommendation for expulsion from the principal, Scott Windham. The expulsions were later changed by the expulsion review committee and superintendent, Roy Breithaupt, to three-day suspensions.

This may have been the end of the matter had it not been for a meeting of some Black students' parents at a local church to discuss how to respond to the situation. Events of this meeting were reported by another local newspaper, the Alexandria *Town Talk*, which referred to the nooses as a "racial incident."[5] According to the *Jena Times*, this began "a constant barrage of negative media coverage" that prompted school officials to describe the incident as "more media hype than reality."[6]

The incident grew into a crisis, and during the following year a large section of the high school was burned, students were intimidated by a local district attorney, and six Black students were charged with attempted murder for the beating of a White student. The latter situation was described by the *Washington Post* as "overzealous prosecution of six black high school students charged with beating a white schoolmate."[7] The situation reached a climax when the "'Jena Six' case Prompt[ed] Mass Demonstrations."[8] It was this prosecution that brought major civil rights leaders, including Jesse Jackson and Al Sharpton, plus thousands of protestors to Jena on September 20, 2007. The crisis was defused in December when the charges against the Black students were reduced substantially from attempted murder to second-degree battery.

Superintendent of schools in the LaSalle Parish's Jena High School, Roy Breithapt, did not view the hanging nooses as indicative of a serious racial incident. He was quoted as saying "in this particular case, I think there is much concern on the part of many people that really has no justification."[9] A child welfare supervisor from the parish who spoke extensively with those students indicated that they did not know about Black history and the hanging of Black citizens during the South's Jim Crow years following the Civil War.

She was quoted as saying "We discussed this in great detail with those students. They honestly had no knowledge of the history concerning nooses and black citizens."[10] These comments were one of the factors considered when the principal's original recommendation for expulsions was reduced by the superintendent to three days of suspensions. Not everyone agreed.

Some Jena citizens saw the Jena hanging nooses as far more serious. A retired administrator from the LaSalle Parish school district commented, "When the superintendent overruled the principal on expulsion, he sent a message that it wasn't that big of a deal to hang such a hateful symbol of racism and terror in a tree at school."[11] Bill Quigley, writing in *Truthout*, quoted a mother of a Jena High student as saying "Hanging those nooses was a hate crime, plain and simple."[12]

The Jena crisis is an example of hidden racism that lurked deep within the culture of Jena High School. The hanging nooses gave it a renewed life and opened a scabbed-over wound. Another instance involving veiled racism occurred in the Coatesville, Pennsylvania school when a series of racial texts that were exchanged between a school district superintendent and the district's athletic director became public. The wound from this 2013 crisis lingers to this day.

A SCHOOL SUPERINTENDENT'S CRISIS

Raw Racism from Supposedly Trusted Leaders

The September 22, 2013, headline in the Sunday *Daily Local News* dramatically read: "CASD in crisis after racially-charged text messages surfaced."[13] This news story featured the school superintendent, Richard Como, and the district's athletic director, James Donato. The account literally shook the southeastern Pennsylvania Coatesville school district with tremors that continue to this day. Here is a printable sampling of the texts (others are too obscene or just plain filthy to include):

> June 4
> Donato to Como—
> "All should just have whatever first names they want . . . then last name is N----R!"(author's note: the "n" word is spelled out in the texts). "Leroy N----r, Preacher N----r, Night train n----r, Clarence n----r, Latoya n----r, Thelma n----r and so on."
> Como to Donato—
> "Great idea! Joe n----r bill n----r snake n----r got a nice ring to it."
> Donato to Como—
> "LMAO!" (author's note: text language for "laughing my a** off").
> Como to Donato
> "hahahahahahahhahahahahaha could have whole homerooms of N----r! hahahahahahaha! Will N----r report to office, pardon the interruption but will N----r report to nurses office. N----r to lunch now!"
> June 7
> Como to Donato (referring to pending teacher lay-offs)
> ". . . 23 get clipped Tuesday . . ."
> Donato to Como—
> "How many n----rs out of 23? Not enough!"
> Como to Donato—
> "Don't know but think it's only 4-5. At most until last minute rush of firing by Goo of Phoenix and Kamara."
> Donato to Como—
> "Good hangings there!"

The ongoing exchange containing sexually explicit remarks regarding interracial sex acts as well as offensive racial, ethnic, and sexual remarks against Blacks, Jews, Arabs, and women continued until June 17, 2013. The texts were especially dramatic considering the school's racially and ethnically diverse student body which in 2014 consisted of 49.6 percent White, 36.1 percent Black, 11.7 percent Hispanic, and 2.6 percent Asian, American Indian, Pacific Islander, or mixed.[14]

The texts came to light after the district's technology director, Abdallah Hawa (referred to in one of the texts as a "camel jockey") was cleansing Donato's district cell phone for reuse after it had been replaced at Donato's request because it was white and therefore too "girly." Deeply upset after he saw some of the texts, Hawa contacted a district administrator who turned it over to a school board member.

The matter remained private until the September 22, *Daily Local News* story brought the matter to the public's attention. The publication resulted in more than 1,000 irate individuals attending the school board meeting on September 25 at which the board had scheduled a vote to accept Como and Donato's resignations. More than three hours of angry, blistering comments made clear the fact that the public wanted the men fired and the entire school board to resign. Ultimately, the board did accept the two resignations citing feared legal problems if Como and Donato were fired outright.[15]

Como and Donato immediately vanished from view. Como still possesses his Pennsylvania superintendent certificate, and both he and Donato are collecting their state pensions. Lawsuits regarding possible misuse of funds that were also mentioned in the texts were resolved when a jury found Como guilty of multiple counts of felony theft on January 26, 2018. Even though new Coatesville superintendents have done much to calm the situation, anger still simmers below the surface more than eight years after the texts were exposed.

The outcry and resentment expressed by employees, students, and the public was generally one of disbelief followed by deep anger. Como had been someone who was admired by most students and residents in the district as he had been a winning high school football coach, assistant principal, and high school principal prior to becoming the superintendent in 2005. One former Coatesville student and past employee (who asked to remain anonymous) had been recommended for his position by Como. She was particularly distraught by the news of the text exchanges and wrote this about the incident:

> Mr. Como was my principal and was very kind to me. I've always had a dream of giving back to my school district and Mr. Como gave me an opportunity to do so. I can't help but wonder if I was just another "N" word to him? With tears in my eyes, as much as I would like to be exempt . . . I'm sure that I'm not. More importantly, this was the face for Coatesville's education? I am so upset and can only pray that God will bless my kids with Administrators [*sic*] and teachers that have their best interest at heart and are not just using them for athletic purposes.[16]

This feeling of betrayal was only one of many that were expressed by confused and exasperated citizens and students. Some but not all professional educators shared similar views.

Some School Leaders Reactions to the Racial Texts

The texts formed the basis for a dialogue in the roundtable sessions at a 2016 Pennsylvania Association of School Administrators' Conference and the

2017 American Association of School Administrators' National Conference. The majority of views expressed were of shock or disbelief. Some, however, indicated that the texts should be viewed as little more than casual locker-room banter or that the real wrongdoing was that the texts were sent on district-owned cell phones. One superintendent commented that had the texts been on private phones their appropriateness would not have been questioned.

Countering this was a comment made by an individual who teaches prospective superintendents at a university near the affected district. She said that a distinction should be made between a person's personality (defined as surface persona) and character (internally held core beliefs). Another superintendent, from a district near a large Midwestern city, commented that if personality and character are not in sync then the outer charade will eventually decay and reveal the internal self.[17] This can lead to individual moral collapse and jeopardize the integrity of the entire school district's professed values. This certainly seems to be the case of the now-infamous superintendent and athletic director.

These later views should cause concern and question whether the Coatesville superintendent is an anomaly or if there are other school leaders among the roughly 14,000 school districts in the United States who might harbor similar prejudices as part of their core values. Participants in the two dialogue round-table sessions expressed their views that there are probably many more superintendents who have similar values. If this is the case then we should try and understand more completely the mindset of individuals who present one face publically while internally harboring dramatically different core values.

Masks that Hide and Reveal

In his book *Emile*, French philosopher Jean Jacques Rousseau describes ways we view ourselves by using the terms *amour de soi* and a*mour de proper*. *Amour de soi* is our authentic self—ways we really see who we are. *Amour de propre* on the other hand is the way we want others to see us—masks that we often wear. Rousseau describes masks this way: "All men wear pretty much the same mask, but . . . there are faces more beautiful than the mask covering them."[18] Considering masks in this context can lead us to a sense of liberation if we can take off our masks and reveal something more beautiful underneath.

The reverse of this can also be true. An article in the *School Administrator* (November 2017), "Combating Hatred Among Us," regarding the Coatesville texting crisis contains a graphic of a mask being removed that reveals a contorted, sinister face behind a more benign mask.[19] Faces behind masks are not always more beautiful than the mask that hides them. Such is the case with the Coatesville racial incident.

Superintendent Como was a hero to many Black students and community members because of his role in coaching winning football teams. He was admired as the high school principal and later district superintendent. The texts revealed another person who, when communicating to his friend Donato, apparently did not feel bound by the social conventions that usually constrained him.

The same may be true of Donato. Both men removed their masks. Their true selves were revealed in the texts, and this revelation uncovered discord between each man's *amour de soi* and *amour de proper*. Their masks were fashioned from what they believed to be politically and socially correct behaviors and attitudes that were accepted in the context of their school community. Como and Donato apparently were friends—at least friendly enough to share these inner feelings.

One of their last text exchanges referred to Black teacher layoffs as "Good hangings there!"[20] This reference brings us back to the deep institutionalized racism that hangings represent in the nooses hanging from the scaffold on January 6, 2021, and from an oak tree at Jena High school. Hanging nooses are a serious matter and ignorance of the history regarding their significance can lead to a disaster for school leaders as well as the entire school districts.

The Jena High School and Coatesville School District crises demonstrate not only a lack of historical knowledge but also the absence of an institutionalized sense of social justice.

A good place to begin gaining an overview of the significance of nooses and lynchings in our history is the National Museum for Peace and Justice, located in Montgomery, Alabama.

INSTITUTIONALIZED RACISM

Deep Significance of Nooses and Lynchings

The National Museum for Peace and Justice is an extremely impactful museum that memorializes the lynchings, burnings, drownings, beatings, and other deaths of 4,400 African Americans between 1877 and 1950. Accompanying the museum is the Legacy Museum that traces the history of racism toward Blacks from enslavement to incarceration. The purpose of the museum, according to words published on its website, is as follows: "The national lynching memorial is a sacred space for truth-telling and reflection about racial terror in America and its legacy."[21]

Research for the memorial and museum began in 2010 and was conducted by members of the Equal Justice Initiative (EJI). The memorial was completed and opened to the public in 2018. EJI staff members researched racially violent deaths, particularly lynchings, which occurred in 800 counties across the United States. The most striking visuals of the memorial are the 800 steel columns representing those counties with the names of the victims engraved on them. A visit to the website is both informative and numbing. See for yourself by going to: https://museumandmemorial.eji.org/memoria.

It is difficult to assess the motives of this type of violence against former slaves without first knowing some of the histories of slavery in America. A brief overview may be helpful.

SOME CONSIDERATIONS OF AMERICAN SLAVERY

Social Control and Institutionalized Racism

The first slaves arrived in 1619 and came initially as indentured servants from different tribes in central Africa. The indentured system quickly died as investors, such as those in the Royal African Company headed by the royal Stuart family, realized that great profits could be made from buying and selling Africans. This trade, part of the triangular trade route (Europe, Africa, and West Indies), flourished until 1807 when the U.S. Congress passed a law prohibiting the importation of slaves.

By its cruelty, the slave trade system guaranteed docility. Africans were captured by hostile tribes or slave hunters. They were stripped, often branded, shackled, and placed in cages called barracoons with other captives who often spoke different languages. Here they waited, sometimes for months, to be jammed onto ships that would take them on the Middle Passage to the West Indies. This brutal voyage lasted anywhere from one to six months depending on the weather. It is estimated that approximately 20 percent of the slaves never survived the Middle Passage.

Once in the West Indies, they were trained for field or other work before being sold to buyers at debasing auctions. The buyers were often representatives of plantation owners located primarily in the United States and Haiti. The slaves in Haiti, led by Toussaint Louverture, revolted against the French and achieved full independence in 1804.

One of the reasons that this revolution is significant is that it struck deep paranoia and fear in southern U.S. slave owners. This led to tightened restrictions which were designed to strengthen social control over American slaves. For example, slaves could not assemble without the presence of a White person, could not learn to read and write, could not own property, and could not marry.

ANTE-BELLUM SOUTH: SOCIAL STRUCTURE

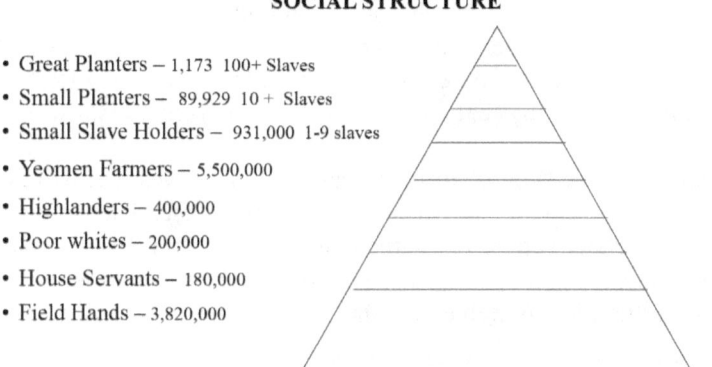

- Great Planters – 1,173 100+ Slaves
- Small Planters – 89,929 10+ Slaves
- Small Slave Holders – 931,000 1-9 slaves
- Yeomen Farmers – 5,500,000
- Highlanders – 400,000
- Poor whites – 200,000
- House Servants – 180,000
- Field Hands – 3,820,000

Figure 2.1 Social Structure of the Antebellum South. *Source*: Author Created.

The need for social control by the slave owners was great as slaves far outnumbered them in the Ante-Bellum South. Here is a visual of the social structure in the Ante-Bellum South[22] (figure 2.1).

In examining the pyramid it can be seen that there were 1,173 Great Planters who are placed in this category because they owned 100 or more slaves. These are the great plantations—*Gone with the Wind*'s Tara or Twelve Oaks—that we often associate with the richness of the Ante-Bellum South. There were 1,020,923 Small Planters and Small Slave Holders. Altogether, then, there were 1,022,102 slave owners. Yeomen farmers account for the bulk of the White population with approximately 5,500,000. The majority of the soldiers who fought for the Confederacy came from this class.

Highlanders—estimated to be 400,000 of the Ante-Bellum Whites—are the ones who refused to secede from the Union and formed the state of West Virginia. Poor Whites, the bottom of the Whites on the pyramid, were those who did not own property and did menial work on the fringes of the plantations. Of the slaves, approximately 180,000 were house servants and 3,820,000 were field hands.

Deeper analysis of these numbers raises important questions. Perhaps the most prominent two are:

- With such overwhelming numbers of slaves to plantation owners (4,000,000 to 1,022,102) why did not a majority of the slaves simply rebel or walk away and follow the North Star across the Ohio River to freedom?
- Why did the Yeomen farmers and Poor Whites support a system of slavery when they themselves did not own slaves?

Perhaps simple answers to these complex questions can be found in the fact that—in addition to beatings, whippings, and other forms of cruelty—docility and social control mentioned earlier had become such powerful forces that rebellion was nearly impossible. As regards the Yeomen farmers, some insight can be gained by realizing that institutionalized racism was firmly in place by 1860.

Concerning Poor Whites, in many cases, some slaves, particularly house servants, were economically better off than they were. The only thing that made them socially superior was the color of their skin. Briefly stated, both Yeomen farmers and Poor Whites fought to keep the social order as it was—it was their culture, it was stable, and they were going to defend it.

SLAVE FREEDOM: WHO WON THE CIVIL WAR?

The Reconstruction period that followed the Civil War (1865–1876) was a time of dramatic changes and hopeful promises for former slaves. The economic, political, and social structure of the Ante-Bellum South was turned, literally, upside down. There was the promise of "forty acres and a mule" for freed slave families to be given from confiscated plantations.[23] Former slaves were elected to legislatures on all levels including the U.S. Congress. These Congresses passed the 13th, 14th, and 15th Amendments to the Constitution which abolished slavery, guaranteed due process to all citizens, and gave the right to vote to former slaves.

The withdrawal of Union troops in 1877 following a political deal over the disputed election of 1876 was the end of Reconstruction. It was also the end of the dreams of former slaves. With the withdrawal of federal troops and diminished fervor for change in the U.S. Congress, economic promises never materialized. Economically, slavery was replaced by tenant farms or sharecropping. This kept former slaves bound in a near-constant state of indebtedness to former slave owners who still owned and controlled the land.

The Civil War amendments quickly decayed, and the political and social controls that were in place in the Ante-Bellum period re-enslaved the great majority of Southern Blacks. Political control of Whites over Blacks was reestablished through such means as poll taxes and literacy tests which were designed to disenfranchise Blacks while leaving Whites untouched.

Social Control was enforced through intimidation by terrifying groups such as the Ku Klux Klan or the Knights of the White Camellia. The Black Codes that kept slaves docile during the Ante-Bellum period were augmented by Jim Crow laws that aimed to keep the White and Black races segregated.[24]

These actions caused prominent scholar of the Civil War and Reconstruction's social history, Harvey Wish, formerly from Case Western

Reserve University, to ask a most important question: "Who Won the Civil War." An excellent history of the Reconstruction period is provided by Henry Louis Gates, Jr.'s *Reconstruction, America after the Civil War* which streams on PBS at (https://www.pbs.org/weta/reconstruction/).

Another powerful study of slavery and its effects is provided by Stanley Elkins's book *Slavery*.[25] It has become a classic interdisciplinary study of American slavery. In this book, Elkins compares aspects of American slavery with the Nazi holocaust. He weaves together history, sociology, economics, and psychology in a manner that sheds a different light on American slavery.

SOME EFFECTS OF INSTITUTIONALIZED RACISM

Segregation of the races has been the most profound and lasting effect of institutionalized racism. Examples permeated the former Confederate states—a few are still in evidence today. These include segregated schools, separate restaurants and hotels, restrooms, and drinking fountains clearly labeled "White" or "Colored" only. While thousands of examples could be given, two in particular, show the depth of segregation and racism. These are of famous Black entertainers Hattie McDaniel and Marian Anderson.

McDaniel won an Oscar for her supporting role of Mammy in *Gone with the Wind*. The Oscar ceremony was held in 1940 at the Ambassador Hotel in Los Angeles. The hotel had a policy that segregated the races. Normally, she would not have been permitted in the Coconut Grove restaurant where the ceremony was held. As a special favor to the producer David O. Selznick, she was placed at a side table along the wall rather than at the *Gone with the Wind* table near the center of the room.

Marian Anderson, an internationally famous opera singer, was not permitted to sing in the Daughters of the American Revolution's Constitutional Hall in Washington because of its segregation policy. This prompted Eleanor Roosevelt to withdraw her membership in the Daughters of the American Revolution and arrange for Marian Anderson to sing on the steps of the Lincoln Memorial.

More than 75,000 spectators heard her open the concert with the words from America—"My country tis of thee, sweet land of liberty, to thee we sing." The contrast of singing about her love of a country whose racism segregated and demeaned her was, and remains, deeply profound. This event should sink deeply into the soul of America. See for yourself on YouTube at https://www.youtube.com/watch?v=XF9Quk0QhSE.

Many educators concerned with racial justice were affected by these and other events that took place mid- and later twentieth century. The following descriptions are of specific responses that educators took to combat institutionalized racial hatred.

EDUCATORS BUILDING BRIDGES ACROSS RACIAL DIVIDES

Experience in Free Form Education (EFFE)

Normandy High School opened in the fall of 1968. It was the newest and most innovative of Parma's three high schools. The principal, Wesley Gaab, and the assistant principal, Marty Kane, were constantly seeking better ways to make learning come alive for more than 2,700 students attending the school in the early 1970s. One of the programs that they initiated was called Experience in Free Form Education or EFFE.[26]

Wes Gaab introduced the EFFE idea to approximately 135 Normandy teachers at a faculty meeting in the fall of 1971. It was an ambitious idea that entailed abolishing the entire high school curriculum for one week and replacing it with hands-on courses conducted both at the school and in the greater community. Teachers could develop courses that they had always wanted to teach but could not because of bureaucratic restraints. Once courses were developed and approved, Gaab and Kane developed an entirely new master schedule and opened registration for students.

Some courses were held in the school and consisted of an extensive array of community and business speakers. Many involved extended trips that incorporated weekends and lasted up to nine days. Examples of these included an in-depth study of theatre in New York City and environmental studies of the Mississippi delta in Louisiana. Others utilized regional community resources such as a course on criminal studies that involved lectures from attorneys and visitations to courtrooms as well as prisons.

Four social studies teachers at Normandy High School developed a course on the city of Cleveland that was designed to provide sociological experiences that students could not get from lectures or textbooks while sitting in their all-White suburban classrooms. This author was one of those teachers. These teachers along with twenty-five students explored the city for five days in unbelievably rich ways.

One of these involved listening to VISTA volunteers in a Hispanic outreach center in Cleveland's near West Side describe why it costs more to be poor. Another was learning about the Bureau of Indian Affairs' policy of assimilation by visiting the Cleveland American Indian Education Center on Denison Avenue. Cleveland's Chinese neighborhood on Rockwell and the Little Italy area centered in Murray Hill near Case Western Reserve University were other sites visited.

One of the speakers in Little Italy shocked most of the group when he described how it was possible to fill the area with armed men from the suburbs in case any Blacks (he used the N word) tried moving into the neighborhood. This comment set a dramatic backdrop for the most memorable encounter—an in-depth visit with Sister Henrietta in the notorious Hough neighborhood—a very depressed section of Cleveland. A description of Sr. Henrietta and her mission is contained in chapter 7.

Camp Confidence

Both insensitivity to racial issues and racial isolation were realities in the Owen J. Roberts School District in the early 1990s. Newstell Marable, head of the local chapter of the National Association for the Advancement of Colored People, had worked for years to get the district to recognize Martin Luther King Day. It was finally recognized as a holiday for students but not employees in the late 1980s. Teachers preferred using this day for in-service so that they could begin summer break one day earlier. It was not until several years later that they reluctantly agreed to honor this day.[27]

Marable was also concerned that many residents in the Park Springs Federal Housing Development felt isolated from the rest of the district. Approximately 5 percent of the district's 3,800 students were classified as African American in 1990. Most of these were concentrated in Park Springs which was located on the outskirts of the district. It was apparent from several comments that many district residents would gladly permit this area to be annexed by the neighboring district—if it wanted them.

To begin changing this attitude meant establishing links with as many Park Springs' students and residents as was possible. Approximately thirty parents and elementary students were gathered at one of the bus stops when a new superintendent drove up and introduced himself to them before boarding the school bus and riding with the students to school. Similar rides were repeated later in the day with middle and high school students.

This move began establishing contacts with several residents that, over the next few weeks, grew into conversations. One conversation that was particularly important occurred with the director of Park Springs, Kevin Lanning. The superintendent had asked Lanning to be his guest at a football game attended by school board members, prominent officials, and other members of the community. While sitting in a reserved section of the home stands, Lanning asked the superintendent if it might be possible to extend the Federal free and reduced school lunch program into the summer. Lightning bolt time—kids are hungry year-round!

More than 95 percent of Park Springs' students were on the Federal free and reduced lunch and breakfast programs. Lanning pointed out something that should have been obvious to everyone—these students needed free nutritious meals year-round and not just for the nine months that school was in session. He then explained that summertime was a real problem for students and other residents of Park Springs.

Federal housing development residents were not permitted to have pets. They could not plant gardens. Playgrounds were essentially barren. As for swimming—the nearest pool was several miles away in Spring City. Youths generally did not have transportation to Spring City nor the daily two-dollar entrance fee. These were serious concerns for Lanning who wondered about the effects of placing students into the pressure cooker of Philadelphia area high temperatures and humidity with inadequate nourishment and little or no physical or mental relief.

These concerns formed the nucleus for a summer camp for students who could not afford to experience a traditional one. The schools had cafeterias, playgrounds, libraries, land for gardens, and a swimming pool—all of which were idle during the summer. Over the next few months several district leaders, school board members, and community residents designed a summer camp for Park Springs and other students who lacked financial resources to attend a traditional summer camp. It began in the summer of 1992 and was called Camp Confidence.

Camp Confidence was a free camp for students who had little, if any, money for a traditional camp experience. To minimize community criticism regarding the expenditure of public monies, no local tax dollars were used to run the camp. Instead, it relied on personal donations of time and money as well as some special state funds that were secured through a grant.

The camp, designed for approximately 100 elementary and middle school-aged youngsters, lasted for approximately six weeks and was held in the district's middle school. It ran from approximately 9:30 in the morning until 2:00 in the afternoon and included a free lunch for the students. The middle school was chosen as the site because it contained a swimming pool and had many unused acres surrounding it. The school's assistant principal agreed to oversee the camp, and certified teachers both within and outside of the district donated their services.

Classroom activities during camp stressed nontraditional approaches to reading and language arts such as puppet theatres, plays, and computer activities. District librarians established a special collection of high-interest books. Physical education teachers designed noncompetitive games for students of different age levels. Field trips were considered of key importance and several focused on environmental and cultural topics. Leadership skills were developed for many participants who in subsequent years became peer counselors for younger campers in the program.

The camp received wide support from school personnel, citizens, and those doing business with the district. One important contribution was from the district's contracted transportation provider who donated daily busses to transport students from Park Springs to the middle school as well as for several field trips during the six-week experience. Other donations included the services of local farmers, organized by a school board member. They plowed plots of land near the middle school so that students could plant individual gardens. The unused pool was put into service with the superintendent teaching swimming at least two days per week

While students were attending the camp, their parents were not forgotten. Strengthening home-school relationships was a core principle of the camp philosophy. One of the conditions for students being able to attend the camp was that their parents agreed to attend various sessions held at Park Springs. These meetings were coordinated by the director of Park Springs and included open discussions led by trained school guidance counselors. They focused on various problems and included discussions on home-school communications, student susceptibility to illegal drugs, problems associated with gang cultures, and other parenting concerns.

The sessions increased parent support for the camp and built a sense of community among participants. This was evident on the "graduation day" when parents and community members attended a special program that recognized each student's contribution to the camp. A brief ceremony was followed by a spaghetti lunch for students, parents, teachers, administrators, school board members, and invited citizens. The lunch was prepared by students with the help of teachers and featured some of the produce that was grown in the campers' gardens.

Camp Confidence was different from most summer school programs that have grown in recent years as a result of various Federal and state programs. There were no pre- or posttests, no scripted programs used by remediation teachers, and no fears of failure. Camp Confidence students developed reading and math skills while having fun-filled active camp experiences designed to bolster their positive self-esteem. They genuinely liked the camp.

One eight-year-old stated in an article in the *Philadelphia Inquirer* that if he was not "attending Camp Confidence, he would be home sleeping or watching TV."[28] These positive sentiments were echoed by a nine-year-old who said "It gives you something to do. I like using the computers. They're fun."[29] Teachers and others associated with the program also felt it was very worthwhile. Camp teachers shared many accounts of the camp with their colleagues during district-wide opening teachers' meetings. One of the farmers who plowed land at the middle school for student gardens was also a school board member. He gave several positive reports on the camp experience at public school board meetings.

Camp Confidence was a bridge across a racial divide that brought Park Springs' students and families more completely into the school district community. The relationships that developed between district personnel, the director, and residents of Park Springs carried over into the regular school year. The camp spurred additional outreach efforts that resulted in elementary after-school programs, ongoing parent meetings, and the installation of a computer lab at Park Springs.

Perhaps the greatest benefit from the Camp Confidence experience was that it opened many people's eyes and created different perspectives regarding the needs of disadvantaged students who were clustered in an isolated section of the district—students who also happened to be mostly African American. Opening eyes and creating new perspectives—this is how "educators buil[t] bridges across racial divides."

SUMMARY: LESSONS LEARNED

- Hanging nooses are indicative of institutionalized racism as seen in the January 6th Capitol riot, the racial crisis in Jena, Louisiana, and in the language of the Coatesville racial exchange.
- Masks people wear often hide true beliefs regarding racial values.
- Educational leaders are often naïve regarding the importance of racial incidents that grow from institutionalized racism.
- Failure of Reconstruction to change the economic political and social structure of the Ante-Bellum South raises the question "Who Won the Civil War."
- The strength of the Black Codes and Jim Crow laws continued to institutionalize racism and provides the basis for radical White supremacist groups today.
- Educators whose sense of social justice can make differences regarding racial isolation and hatred by building bridges across racial divides.

The hanging noose was only one of the many racist symbols to appear at the Capitol on January 6. A sweatshirt blaring the name of the notorious death camp, Auschwitz, was boldly on display as well. "The Power of Symbols: Auschwitz" is the title of the next chapter in our quest to combat hatred for the soul of America. After a consideration of the Auschwitz sweatshirt at the January 6 riot, the chapter will focus on anti-Semitism in general and a particular confrontation regarding Christian prayer at a graduation ceremony when the valedictorian was a young Jewish woman.

NOTES

1. Jill Colivn, "Capitol mob built gallows and chanted 'Hang Mike Pence,'" *Associated Press, Quad Cities,* https://www.ourquadcities.com/news/national-news

/capitol-mob-built-gallows-and-chanted-hang-mike-pence/ (accessed August 28, 2021).

2. "Incident more hype than reality," *Jena Times*, September 13, 2006, 1, https://www.google.com/search?q=jena+times+september+13,+2006&tbm=isch&source=iu&ictx=1&fir=MpCwU1hi0akKCM%252CmivrWQ1tHw5iEM%252C_&vet=1&usg=AI4_-kTVCnYreqp (accessed August 29, 2021).

3. Michael Price and Kristina Scala, "CASD in crisis after racially-charged text messages surface," *Daily Local News*, September 22, 2013, 1.

4. Andrew Caballero-Reynolds, "A Noose is seen on makeshift gallows as supporters of Donald Trump gather outside the Capitol, Photograph: /AFP/Getty Images," *The Guardian*, January 10, 2021, https://www.theguardian.com/us-news/2021/jan/10/hang-mike-pence-twitter-stops-phrase-trending-capitol-breach (accessed August 29, 2021).

5. Bill Sumrall, "Jena High noose incident triggers parental protests," *Town Talk*, September 6, 2006.

6. Ibid., *Incident more hype*, 1.

7. Peter Whoriskey, "Thousands protest Blacks' treatment," *The Washington Post*, September 21, 2007, http://www.washingtonpost.com/wp-dyn/content/article/2007/09/20/AR2007092000259_pf.html (accessed December 28, 2017).

8. Audie Cornish, "'Jena Six' case prompts mass demonstrations," *NPR*, September 20, 2007, http://www.npr.org/templates/story.php?storyLd=14574972 (accessed November 15, 2017).

9. Ibid., *Incident more hype*, 2.

10. "Chronological order of events concerning the 'Jena Six,'" *Jena Times* www.thejenatimes.nte/home-page-graphics/home.html. This quotation is taken from a publication titled "Chronological Order of Events Concerning the 'Jena Six'" that was prepared by the editor and staff of the *Jena Times* on an ongoing basis between August 30, 2006, and December 4, 2007. It was accessed by the author from the URL provided above on February 22, 2008. This site is no longer functioning, and the "Chronological Order of Events Concerning the 'Jena Six,'" is no longer on the *Jena Times* home page. The URL and article have been referenced several times by respected national news organizations such as the *New York Times* and the *Christian Science Monitor*. A hard copy of "Chronological Order of Events Concerning the 'Jena Six,'" is in the author's files.

11. Lesli A. Maxwell, "'Jena Six': Case study in racial tensions," September 28, 2007, https://www.edweek.org/ew/articles/2007/10/03/06jena.h27.html (accessed December 30, 2017).

12. Bill Quigley, "Injustice in Jena as Nooses Hang from the 'White Tree,'" http://truth-out.org/archive/component/k2/item/71606:bill-quigley--injustice-in-jena-as-nooses-hang-from-the-white-tree (accessed February 14, 2018).

13. Ibid., Price and Scala, "CASD in crisis after racially-charged."

14. School Digger, Coatesville Area School District, http://www.schooldigger.com/go/PA/schools/0624005012/school.aspx (accessed January 26, 2016).

15. Michael Price and Kristina Scala, "Coatesville School Board allows two execs to resign after racist texts; public fumes," *Daily Local News*, September 25, 2013, 1.

16. Private communication from Korey Bell, Counselor, Henderson High School to Terrance Furin, February 3, 2014.

17. This book's author chaired the roundtables at both the Pennsylvania Association of School Administrators and the American Association of School Administrators' conferences. Comments are based on notes taken from those conferences.

18. Jean-Jacques Rousseau, *Emile or on Education*, ed., trans., Allan Bloom (New York: Basic Books, 1979), 237.

19. Terrance Furin, "Combating hatred among us," *School Administrator*, November, 2017, 43.

20. Ibid., Price and Scala, September 22, 2013.

21. The National Memorial for Peace and Justice, https://museumandmemorial.eji.org/ (accessed August 29, 2021).

22. The material for this pyramid has come from lectures given at Case Western Reserve University by Harvey Wish, prominent writer and lecturer on slavery and American social history. See https://case.edu/ech/articles/w/wish-harvey for more information on Wish.

23. For a brief overview of this unkept promise, see at https://www.pbs.org/wnet/african-americans-many-rivers-to-cross/history/the-truth-behind-40-acres-and-a-mule/.

24. For a brief description and history of the term "Jim Crow," see https://www.ferris.edu/htmls/news/jimcrow/origins.htm.

25. Stanley Elkins, *Slavery* (Chicago: The University of Chicago Press, 1968).

26. Note: author Terrance Furin was member of the Normandy faculty. Information in this section is taken from notes and conversations with former colleagues.

27. Note: author Terrance Furin was superintendent of Owen J. Roberts from 1990 until 2001.

Information in this section is taken from notes and conversations with former colleagues.

28. Susan Weidner, "Summertime and the schooling is easy," *Philadelphia Inquirer*, July 14, 1994, B1.

29. Ibid.

Chapter 3

The Power of Symbols

Auschwitz, Anti-Semitism, and a School Prayer Crisis

Sobibor—167,000
Chelmno—167,000
Belzec—434,000
Treblinka—925,000
Auschwitz—1,000,000

AUSCHWITZ IN THE NATION'S CAPITOL: HERD MENTALITY

"Camp Auschwitz"

Two million, six-hundred and ninety-four thousand (2,694,000) is the approximate number of Jews exterminated by Nazis at the five death camps listed above. They are only part of the estimated six million killed not for what they did but for who they were. Auschwitz not only has the greatest number but also is the most notorious.[1]

A demonstrator at the January 6, 2021, Capitol riot wore a black sweatshirt with the large inscription "CAMP AUSCHWITZ" in white lettering above a skull and crossbones. Beneath the skull is a smaller inscription "work brings freedom," a translation of German iron-lettering *arbeit macht frei*, which hung over the main entrance to the death camp in Nazi-occupied Poland. On the back of the shirt was the word "Staff."[2] The fifty-six-year-old man boldly wearing the shirt, Robert Keith Parker of Newport News, Virginia, was arrested on January 13 for his role in the riot.[3]

The word "Auschwitz" has become one of the most dreaded symbols of the hatred that lies deep within the cultures that led to both the death camps and the January 6 riot. Other symbols were also violently exhibited on January 6. Among them were Q (Q Anon), a hanging noose, the Gadsden Flag (Don't Tread on me), and the Three-Percenter Flag.[4]

These symbols and flags represent various hate groups. The Sothern Poverty Law Center (SPLC) defines a hate group as "an organization or collection of individuals that—based on its official statements or principles, the statements of its leaders, or its activities—has beliefs or practices that attack or malign an entire class of people, typically for their immutable characteristics."[5] One of the most notable characteristics of these hate groups is their intense sense of community. A strong sense of community can be a goal in and of itself. More importantly, it can be a process to achieve goals based upon the ethos of the community.

As a process, a strong sense of community can be powerful in achieving lofty goals. It can also be a powerful force in spreading hatred and "maligning an entire class of people." This is precisely what the wearing of an "Auschwitz" sweatshirt does as regards Jews and the Nazi attempts to annihilate all of them. This leads to a type of mentality wherein entire races, religions, nationalities, and ethnic groups are not considered as groups comprised of unique individuals but rather as faceless numbers in a generalized mass. In this instance, the term "herd mentality" can be appropriately applied.

Another shirt, seen at a demonstration in Washington on December 12, 2020, protesting Biden's election victory exemplifies this herd mentality. Worn by a member of the Proud Boys, it proclaimed above a fascist eagle that "6MWE"—6 Million Wasn't Enough. This refers to the estimated number of Jews exterminated by the Nazis.[6] Helping to provide some insight into the dreadful terrors of the Holocaust and herd mentality is Gitta Sereny's book *Into That Darkness*: *An Examination of Conscience*.

Into That Darkness

Gitta Sereny's relentless research and careful writing help to penetrate some of the dense darkness of hatred found at Nazi death camps. She interviewed Franz Stangl who was commandant of the death camps Sobibor (April–August 1942) and Treblinka (September 1942–August 1943). Sereny interviewed him for more than seventy hours while he was serving a life sentence in Düsseldorf. The final interview was conducted just nineteen hours before his death of heart failure in 1971. She verified his answers with interviews from, among others, his wife, accomplices at the death camps, friends, and some victims.

Through her interviews, Sereny presents a picture of Stangl as a complex human through his various interactions. In describing Sereny's book, Elie Wiesel wrote the following powerful sentences.

It is not the murderer in Stangl that terrifies us—it is the human being. For that matter "terrify" may not be the right word. Most often one is sick to one's soul. Yes, that is the word needed, a word from Sartre—one is gripped by a profound existential nausea.[7]

Stangl contended that while at both Sobibor and Treblinka his duties were strictly administrative. Yes, he knew of the gassings and burnings of hundreds of thousands of Jews. Yes, he was aware of first the stripping and then the whippings so as to direct cowered masses into the tunnel (tube) that led to their deaths. Yes, he knew that the arrival of thousands crammed into boxcars meant the end of their lives. But on the other hand, was not he the one who oversaw the construction of a model train station complete with a fake clock and flower beds so that victims could feel more at ease on their arrival before making their way to the gassings?

Throughout her interviews, Sereny kept politely yet skillfully probing Stangl to try and find what it was that enabled him to be in charge of ruthless death camps and at the same time be a tender and gentle husband, father and friend to so many. An exchange during one particular interview seemed to provide at least a partial explanation. Stangl described an episode when a train he was riding while on leave to see his wife stopped next to a slaughterhouse. He described the animals who were very close to his window, looking up at him, and said it reminded him of his times in Poland (Treblinka).

Sereny pressed him in this exchange:

Sereny: "So you didn't feel they were human beings?"
Stangl: "Cargo" he said tonelessly. "They were cargo."
Sereny: "When do you think that you began to think of them as cargo?"
Stangl: "I think that it started the day I first saw the *totenlager* [toten—death; lager—warehouse] in Treblinka. I remember Wirth standing there, next to the pits full of blue-black corpses. It had nothing to do with humanity—it couldn't have; it was a mass—a mass of rotting flesh. Wirth said, what shall we do with this garbage?"
Sereny: "There were so many children, did they ever make you think of your children, of how you would feel in the position of those parents?"
Srangl: "No" . . . "I can't say I ever thought that way." . . . You see, I rarely saw them as individuals. It was always a huge mass. I sometimes stood on the wall and saw them in the tube. But—how can I explain it—they were naked packed together, running, being driven with whips.[8]

"Auschwitz" on a sweatshirt in the Nation's Capitol? Herd mentality, indeed. Let us individualize and personalize what seeing that shirt emblazoned with that word meant to two survivors of Nazi atrocities.

Reactions from Survivors: Personalizing the Mass Atrocities

Eva Umlauf was a toddler when freed from Auschwitz in 1945. She still bears the numbers Nazis tattooed on her arm—A-26959. Though young at the time, memories of the atrocities were passed on to her from her mother who was also a survivor. The Auschwitz inscription on the sweatshirt troubled her deeply. She is quoted as saying: "I couldn't believe what I was seeing . . . I never would have believed that was possible from Americans."[9] Regarding other images from that day she stated: "They [rioters] trampled on democratic principles in the heart of democracy."[10]

Eva Umlauf is more than numbers tattooed on an arm. She is a name and a face—indeed, much more than that. She went to medical school, became a pediatrician, married, and has three sons. She is one of the fortunate Jews who survived the Holocaust. Many who were not Jewish were also terrorized or enslaved. Such is the story of Joseph (Joe) Brozozowski who this author knows personally and considers him to be a friend. This relationship provides a window into more than a Polish boy who was enslaved—it gives a glimpse into one of the victim's souls.

This author met Joe at a breakfast with a small group of parishioners following an early weekday Catholic mass just prior to the 2019–2021 pandemic. Joe is a very active man, certainly seeming much younger than his eighty-six years. As the breakfast conversation grew beyond initial pleasantries, he talked about his being a grandfather, author, artist, and cook who specializes in Polish favorites such as *gołąbki* and *pierogi*. He also is an avid reader who especially likes history books. The cheerful glint in his eye grew dimmer as he revealed his past as a survivor of both a Nazi concentration camp and an enslaved labor.[11]

Joe survived Bergen-Belsen—the camp notorious for the death of Anne Frank—and much more. In 1943, at the age of nine, he was rounded up with other members of his Polish family and shipped to the camp which was being used at that time to hold prisoners. He said that being Polish, and not Jewish, probably saved his life. Rather than being exterminated, he and some members of his family were transferred to a small farm as slave laborers for the duration of the war.

In 1945, he was liberated by British forces who detained him in camps for Displaced Persons (DPs) for approximately four years. It was during this time that he learned English (in addition to his native Polish and acquired German) in schools established by the British for DPs. He considered his education to be exceptional, often being taught by professors from prestigious universities such as Oxford. Being a DP, Joe was eligible to come to the United States. He was sponsored by the Catholic War Relief Agency and became a worker on a dairy farm in Arkansas. Life on the farm was tough mainly because of the cruelty of the farm's owner.

Joe was obligated to remain on the dairy farm for one year, but with the intervention of a local priest, he was relocated to a rice farm where he stayed for the next two years. Being a talented artist he had dreams of going to New York's Pratt Institute. He could not afford the cost and settled for a supermarket job while attending vocation school to become an electrician. He became an electrician for Anaconda Copper until 1966 when he began a thirty-one career as a highly skilled technician at Johnson and Johnson.

Joe's brief biography is shared because, similar to Eva, it puts human depth to his remarks concerning the January 6 Capitol riot. His words are from someone who deeply loves this country, and they come from his heart and soul.

Here they are:

> It is our eternal struggle, as humans, [not] to repeat the dark times of our history. On January 6, 2021, the Capitol Building was attacked by a mob; their goal, to destroy our free democratic election process.
>
> I sat in my living room and my visual memory came back from my childhood when my family was taken by train from eastern Poland to northern Germany. In June of 1943 we were taken, by box car, to the concentration camp in Bergen-Belsen. Bergen-Belsen was a prison camp, which later became a death camp. My family spent two weeks in the camp, then we were sent as slave labor to work a farm in a village near Rotenburg. In 1945 we were liberated by the British forces.
>
> As I watched the insurrection of our nation I saw one man in the mob wearing a t-shirt with the word AUSCHWITZ printed on it (the concentration camp at Auschwitz was the location where 1.2 million human souls were exterminated by a terrible death). This man, one among several hundred ... defaced our capital. I could not comprehend why this mob would support ... [anyone] who was akin to a dictator, the likes of Putin or Hitler.[12]

Eva and Joe's reactions throw unique, individualized humanness onto the Auschwitz symbol. As such these personalized accounts combat the herd mentality epitomized by Stangl's words.

Let us now turn to a practical example of a school superintendent who individualized and confronted anti-Semitic hatred that arose over Christian prayer at a Commencement ceremony.

CHRISTIAN PRAYER AND ANTI-SEMITISM AT A HIGH SCHOOL COMMENCEMENT

Many may assume that by the early 1990s the Constitutional controversies regarding school prayer had been clarified by the U.S. Supreme Court. Key decisions in 1962 (*Engel v. Vitale*), 1963 (*Abington School District v.*

Schempp), and 1971 (*Lemon v. Kurtzman*) made it apparent that the First Amendment's separation of church and state extended to the nation's public schools. The crisis at Owen J. Roberts demonstrated that there is often a great divide between decisions reached in Washington and local practice.

Commencement Prayer Eliminated

She was a young Jewish woman in a public school district dominated by Christian fundamentalists. Nineteen-ninety was her senior year, and because she had the highest grade-point average she was chosen as valedictorian of her class. Most people would never have known that she was Jewish had it not been for the required baccalaureate held prior to graduation. Following years of tradition, the service was heavy with Christian preaching. She and her family found the service not a source of pride but deeply offensive.

Hoping to avoid similar distress at the commencement where she would speak three days later, the family approached the high school principal and asked whether Christian prayer was also on that program. When told that it was, they, with the aid of the American Civil Liberties Union (ACLU), filed suit in the Eastern District Federal Court and were granted a restraining order against prayer at the graduation ceremony. The community erupted with outrage.

One resident reportedly said, "It's terrible . . . you're taking one person's freedom of speech and stopping 200 others."[13] An editorial in the most popular of the local newspapers stated that the decision "smacks of fanaticism."[14] The editorial was accompanied by a cartoon depicting an ACLU lawyer as tolerant of abusive free speech in movies and rock music while attempting to muzzle a clergyman.[15]

This outcry set the stage for a conflict over freedom of religious expression that rocked this school district of nearly 4,000 students. The situation was made worse by a transfer of power between two superintendents that left a leadership vacuum for the school board. Feeling pressure from the community, the board began preparing to fight the Federal court's decision. As the new superintendent, I had other plans.

Taking a Stand

The outgoing superintendent's advice was to lie low on the prayer issue.[16] This did not seem to be an option for the new superintendent as various U.S. Supreme Court decisions seemed to protect students' rights to individualized religious beliefs. They also recognized the important principle separating church and state in public schools. To fight the Christian fundamentalists by supporting the ACLU's ban on school prayer would be a daunting task.

The administrative team—principals, assistant principals, and central office administrators—would need to be united.

For this reason, various members of that team researched school prayer rulings with their different professional organizations and together developed a policy that eliminated prayer at all school-sponsored events. The school board considered the policy before a hostile crowd of nearly 500 citizens at a meeting prior to the start of the new school year. Philadelphia's major television stations, the *Philadelphia Inquirer*, and four local newspapers captured images of angry citizens demanding that the board defeat the proposed policy.

Leading the outcry was a representative from the Rutherford Institute who offered his services to fight the prayer ban all the way to the Supreme Court. After more than two hours of angry comments, the board voted unanimously to approve the new policy. Chaos broke out in the auditorium. Above the pandemonium were heard shouts of "chickens," "yellow-bellies," and "you're running scared."[17]

The wrath of the Christian fundamentalists fell squarely on the new superintendent. He was stalked at his residence, had trash stolen, was called the anti-Christ and Satan, received intimidating letters that warned of burning in hell, and was investigated by a private detective. His family, still residing in Ohio, was threatened as well. His youngest daughter, a high school freshman at the time, was questioned by authorities because someone anonymously reported him to children's services as a child abuser.

These hateful acts made it tempting for the new superintendent to leave the district, but the issue was too important to leave. This obstinacy increased the anger and it became directed at the school board. One man's irate letter to a local newspaper captured the mood of many regarding the board when he wrote, "From their vote it's obvious that the current OJR School Board is comprised of a group of gutless wonders who are unresponsive to the wishes of the majority of taxpayers."[18]

Five of the nine school board seats were up for election the following year. Several Christian fundamentalists began a coordinated effort to capture a majority of these. Their campaign drew national attention and became a model across the country.

Wrath against the School Board: A Stealth Campaign

Four new school directors were elected following a political campaign that an article in *Education Week* cited as a "stealth campaign."[19] This term mobilized the political strategy used by a team of Christian fundamentalists who on the surface ran as separate individuals. It was only after the election that a national organization known as the National Association of Christian Educators/Citizens for Excellence in Education (often referred to simply as CEE) proclaimed that a "Tremendous Victory in School Board Race" had occurred in this district and that the individual winners had in reality run as a team.[20]

CEE's *Education Newsline*, sent to the organizations 868 chapters, declared the victory in this local school board election as "nothing short of a miracle."[21] In this same newsletter, one of the newly elected local school directors outlined the plan that the Christian fundamentalist team had followed. Key elements explained in this plan included these tactics:

- The team found a committed Christian who was willing to take the reins of managing the campaign and did not make any decisions unless it was cleared through him.
- The team emphasized running individually and not as a slate yet met regularly to plan campaign strategies.
- A few days before the election, the team advertised that each individual was supported by an amorphous committee, in this case called the Citizens for Responsive Education, which would help voters link the names together.
- The week before the election, each candidate called voter lists, scheduled cottage prayer meetings, and on the eve of the election held a large prayer rally for supporters.[22]

The plan worked. It is little wonder that Robert Simonds, head of CEE, was boastful. He wrote in a *President's Report* soon after the election that "We have meticulously followed God's plan and His biblical principles . . . to redeem America's children from the clutches of atheism, immorality, and psychological brainwashing."[23]

The board was now badly divided. This made it difficult if not impossible for the board/administrative team to provide leadership for the school district. The community itself was also deeply divided. Hatred based on intolerance had turned into vengeance.

Combating the Crisis: Dialoguing Great Literature over Breakfast

Quick and decisive actions were needed if there was any hope of creating an atmosphere in which the board and administration could find common ground for working together. This was a necessary first step toward bridging the deep divisions within the community. To this end, the administrative leadership team scheduled a series of orientation meetings over the next several months that were designed to deal with topics such as school finance, curriculum, personnel procedures, policy development, and other matters. The first of these meetings would be the most important as it would be the initial meeting between new and former board members.

This meeting was not planned to deal with routine matters or school board procedures. It was designed to begin a conversation that would lead to the board becoming a community of learners where the inherent equality and dignity of each person would be acknowledged. Ernest Hemingway, the literary giant, helped begin this conversation. His classic *The Old Man and the Sea* was the focus for the first meeting, a dialogue session, scheduled for 8:00 a.m. on a cold and snowy Saturday morning in January.

The dialogue session started with a candlelight breakfast for nine board members and three central office administrators. In preparation for the session, each participant was given a copy of Ernest Hemingway's 1952 novel *The Old Man and the Sea*. This book by the Nobel Prize–winning author was chosen because it was not only a quick read but was also profoundly simple and at the same time very deep. Everyone was asked to read it beforehand, and they all did arrive with books in hand.

The breakfast, candles, and soft background music from *Out of Africa* proved to be somewhat of an icebreaker even though individuals clustered together in groupings with known colleagues. This soon changed when everyone assembled around a large table and began a conversation by considering Hemingway's use of color in the novel.

The reflection on color was begun by reading a quotation from the novel in which Hemingway described the first time that the old man, Santiago, saw the giant fish that he caught on his third day far out at sea. Hemingway painted with vivid colors this way: "He was bright in the sun and his head and back were dark purple and in the sun the stripes on his sides showed wide and a light lavender."[24] Following that reading, everyone was asked to reflect privately on what color they would choose to describe the entire novel.

After several minutes, each person presented a color and explained what it meant to them. Dialogue between supposed adversaries began. There could be no right or wrong answers, and individuals learned much about each other by responding to the question.

Following this activity, individuals began to focus on three themes in the novel—heroism, man and nature (harmony or conflict), and spiritual symbolisms. Individuals were assigned one of the themes, and after some quiet time during which they sought ideas from the novel relative to their theme, three groups were formed. The groupings were prearranged to contain new and former board members plus an administrator who served as a facilitator. Individuals shared their thoughts and findings with other members of their group for about thirty minutes. They then chose a spokesperson to summarize the group's dialogue for everyone else.

While each group presented interesting commentaries, the most memorable came from the spiritual symbolism group. The spokesperson for this group was the minister who was the person chosen to give the invocation at the notorious commencement. Now, as one of the newly elected board members, he presented many examples of spiritual symbols from the novel.

One of these was the importance of the number three. For example, Santiago (Spanish for Saint James) had to endure three nights before hooking the marlin. He compared this with the New Testament importance of the number three as in Jesus's resurrection on the third day and the theological significance of the trinity. Other illustrations included Santiago's occupation as a fisherman, his loneliness at being abandoned and his frequent prayers.

The most poignant of the examples was the board member's comparison of the crucifixion of Jesus with the scene near the end of the novel in which Hemingway described Santiago falling several times while climbing a hill to his shack with the mast of the skiff across his shoulders. This scene unfolded with a background of the white bones of the marlin's skeleton still attached to the skiff, bobbing in the water—a reminder of the prophet Ezekiel's description of the valley of dry bones.

This board member spoke with deep feelings that charged the atmosphere in the room for several silent moments after he finished speaking. Everyone felt deeply moved. It was truly a transcendent experience that testified to the power of dialogue.

In summarizing the morning's experiences, participants came to realize that they had come together and had acted as a community of learners. On the blackboard, each board member was asked to list behaviors that were considered fair or acceptable to be a member of such a community of learners. This is a summary of their list of acceptable behaviors:

- attendance,
- preparation,
- participation,
- open-mindedness,
- a willingness to share both thoughts and feelings,
- being a good listener,
- respecting the views of others,
- focusing on ideas rather than individuals,
- constructive criticism,
- objectivity,
- common courtesy,
- honesty,
- a willingness to accept majority views,
- being up-front, and
- enthusiasm.

Each person was asked to review the list and object if there was anything with which they could not agree. Everyone accepted the list and agreed that it would become a type of contract for future interactions. Even though there were times over the next few years that the board and central office administrators needed to review the agreed-upon behaviors, it proved to be a remarkably durable accord.

During the six months following *The Old Man and the Sea* session, the board met with key administrators seventeen times beyond their regularly scheduled public meetings for in-service sessions that dealt with practical matters such as school board policies and procedures. These sessions proved to be important as they strengthened the relationships that had begun during the Saturday dialogue session. As important as these sessions were, the most important meeting was their initial encounter where open communications based upon honest dialogue helped nine board members and central office administrators find common ground where they could respect each other and begin working together for the benefit of the district's students.

The ideas of two prominent educational theorists are demonstrated in that Saturday dialogue session. One of these is Maxine Greene and her thoughts regarding aesthetics. The other is Alexander Sidorkin and his concepts of dialogue.

THEORY AND PRACTICE: AESTHETIC EXPERIENCES AND AUTHENTIC DIALOGUE

Maxine Greene, former professor at Columbia University's Teachers College, is a leading educational theorist regarding the importance of aesthetic experiences. She was a pupil of John Dewey's and similar to him advocated the strong position that aesthetics should hold in a progressive educational philosophy.

Greene has written numerous books that make known her passion regarding the potential that various art forms have in creating new perspectives and enriched learning experiences. In *Variations on a Blue Guitar*, she wrote that following an aesthetic encounter "we experience a sense of surprise oftentimes, an acute sense that things may look otherwise, feel otherwise, *be* otherwise than we have assumed—and suddenly the world seems new, with possibilities still to be explored (emphasis in original)."[25]

Gaining new perspectives can bring people together and help them dream. Maxine Greene believes that aesthetic experiences can make this happen more readily. She wrote in *Landscapes for Learning*,

> I would want to see one or another art form taught in all pedagogical contexts, because of the way in which aesthetic experiences provide a ground for the

questioning that launches sense-making and the understanding of what it is to exist in a world.²⁶

Ernest Hemingway's powerful writing caused the participants to "experience a sense of surprise"²⁷ and have an encounter with each other in which they looked at things differently and became something other than they had assumed prior to the session. The dialogue session helped them further by "launch[ing] sense-making and the understanding of what it [was] to exist in a world."²⁸ Though it was probably not his intended purpose, Ernest Hemingway helped these diverse individuals find common ground on which they began to build a community of learners.

Alexander Sidorkin's thoughts concerning dialogue also provide a theoretical understanding of *The Old Man and the Sea* session. Sidorkin offers insights into the term "dialogue" that has become a popular expression among managers in both education and the corporate world. Many of these managers see dialogue as a process to gain support for various proposals or to build coalitions for organizational goals. Used in these ways, dialogue is oftentimes not free-flowing or democratic but represents, instead, a process to rubber-stamp preconceived views. A better word to use in these cases would be "discussion" a percussive term, which differentiates it from more authentic dialogue.

Raymond Horn, a prominent educational leadership theorist formerly at Saint Joseph's University in Philadelphia, probed deeply into the meaning of the term dialogue in his article "Differing Perspectives on the Magic of Dialogue: Implications for a Scholar-Practitioner Leader" that appeared in a 2002 issue of *Scholar Practitioner Quarterly*. His work is especially important in distinguishing the difference between a systems' approach to dialogue often used in an organizational context and dialogue founded upon true democratic principles.

Horn described the importance of a leader being a scholar-practitioner and connected such a leader with the importance of democratic dialogue. He wrote that "scholar-practitioner leaders are active agents in human affairs, and therefore recognize the primacy of conversation, especially when agreement needs to be reached among groups with divergent positions."²⁹

After establishing the importance of dialogue for scholar-practitioners, Horn presents four different perspectives of dialogue through a review of books by Elizabeth Ellsworth (*Teaching Positions: Difference, Pedagogy, and the Power of Address*), William Isaacs (*Dialogue and the Art of Thinking Together*), Daniel Yankelovich (*The Magic of Dialogue: Transforming Conflict into Cooperation*), and Alexander Sidorkin (*Beyond Discourse: Education, the Self, and Dialogue*).

Horn contends that two of these authors, Isaacs and Yankelovich, develop dialogue theories in the context of organizational management systems. Both of these see dialogue as important in leading to anticipated understandings. This approach is not essentially democratic, and Horn criticizes it this way, "However, in both cases, the anticipated understanding will not significantly recognize the inherent difference between the participants, and will pressure some participants to suppress their ideas and feelings in order to promote dialogic coherence and continuity."[30]

Horn finds support for his belief regarding such management systems' approaches in Elizabeth Ellsworth's writing. According to him, she supports his view as she sees most dialogues as attempts to impose controlling values, especially those of the leader who has arranged for the dialogue session. He finds similar support from Alexander Sidorkin whose views on dialogue are based upon core democratic values. It is Sidorkin's views that resonate most completely with the Saturday dialogue session on Hemingway's *The Old Man and the Sea*.

Sidorkin's concept of dialogue is far more attuned with human rather than organizational qualities. He wrote that "We are human in the fullest sense when we engage in dialogue."[31] He contends further that dialogue is not a process or means to accomplish some other aim. It by itself is the goal. He stated this concept as follows: "Dialogue is an end in itself, the very essence of human existence."[32] This conception of dialogue requires a democratic context in which all beings are viewed with inherent equality and dignity. Within such a context it is possible to relate fully with another human being. When this relationship occurs, important dialogue happens. This relationship, in Sidorkin's words, "takes you completely out of your regular life."[33]

A greater understanding of the dynamics of the Saturday dialogue session emerges when we couple Sidorkin's views of dialogue with the Maxine Greene's ideas regarding the importance of aesthetic experiences. Creating dialogue itself was the goal of the Saturday session, and Hemingway's novel proved to be an effective art form through which to establish it within a democratic context. Open communications and honest dialogue helped move perceived adversaries onto the common ground where they respected the genuine importance of each other as human beings.

SUMMARY: LESSONS LEARNED

This chapter has explored the power of symbols as seen in the Auschwitz sweatshirt's anti-Semitic expression, the concept of herd mentality and the practical example of a school superintendent's confrontation of anti-Semitism. Some lessons learned from these experiences are the following:

- A knowledge of history, particularly regarding human rights and social justice for all members of a society, is essential in combating hatred.

- Hatred is often based upon a herd mentality that does not view the uniqueness and beauty of each human being.
- A strong sense of personal agency and courage as seen in the Jewish valedictorian's discomfort and unwillingness to accept a situation that ran counter to her core beliefs is essential to combating hatred.
- Interdisciplinary approaches can turn potentially hostile confrontations into opportunities for creating deep and productive dialogue rather than merely percussive discussions based upon preconceived ideas and prejudices.

With these lessons in mind let us turn next to chapter 4, "Neo-Nazis and a Proposed School-wide Boycott." Here we will learn about a school district crisis that occurred when a group of neo-Nazis circulated a recruitment flyer which called for a school-wide boycott to honor Heinrich Himmler, head of the dreaded Nazi SS troops. Led by high school teachers, the community came together and formed several unity coalitions to combat this form of hatred. This powerful example of public pedagogy was institutionalized in a foundation dedicated to combating hatred such as that presented by the neo-Nazis.

NOTES

1. Documenting Numbers of Victims of the Holocaust, https://encyclopedia.ushmm.org/content/en/article/documenting-numbers-of-victims-of-the-holocaust-and-nazi-persecution (accessed August 7, 2021).

2. Laura Adkins and Emily Burack, "Capitol riots: What far-right hate symbols were on display?" *The Jerusalem Post*, January 8, 2021, https://www.jpost.com/diaspora/antisemitism/capitol-riots-what-far-right-hate-symbols-were-on-display-654694 (addressed August 8, 2021).

3. David K. Li and Shamar Walters, "Man in 'Camp Auschwitz' shirt, photographed at U.S. Capitol riot arrested in Virginia," *NBC News*, January 13, 2021, https://www.nbcnews.com/news/us-news/man-camp-auschwitz-shirt-photographed-u-s-capitol-riot-arrested-n1254070 (accessed August 8, 2021).

4. Dena Zaru, "The symbols of hate and far-right extremism on display in pro-Trump Capitol siege," *ABC News*, January 14, 2021, https://abcnews.go.com/US/symbols-hate-extremism-display-pro-trump-capitol-siege/story?id=75177671 (accessed August 13, 2021).

5. Southern Poverty Law Center definition of a hate group, https://www.splcenter.org/20200318/frequently-asked-questions-about-hate-groups#hate%20group (accessed July 22, 2021).

6. Alan Kaspark, "Is '6MWE' an anti-semitic proud boys slogan?" December 18, 2020, https://www.snopes.com/fact-check/proud-boy-6mwe/ (accessed August 14, 2021).

7. Elie Wiesel, back cover of Gitta Sereny, *Into That Darkness: An Examination of Conscience* (New York: Vintage Books, 1974).

8. Gitta Sereny, *Into That Darkness: An Examination of Conscience* (New York: Vintage Books, 1974), 201.

9. Melissa Eddy, "Amid the rampage at the U.S. capitol, a sweatshirt stirs troubling memories," *The New York Times*, January 8, 2021, https://www.nytimes.com/2021/01/08/world/europe/us-capitol-rampage-camp-auschwitz.html (accessed August 10, 2021).

10. Ibid.

11. Information regarding Joseph Brozozowski comes from various conversations and interviews with Terrance Furin from August 2019 to September 2021.

12. Joseph Brozozowski, written quotation given to Terrance Furin on August 9, 2021.

13. Debra Noell, "At OJR the graduates didn't have a prayer," *The Mercury*, June 14, 1990, 8.

14. Editorial, "U.S. supreme court attempts to deny our spiritual heritage," *The Mercury*, June 24, 1990, A10.

15. Ibid.

16. Roy Claypool and Terrance Furin, personal communication, June 15, 1990.

17. Derrick Gray, "OJR passes prayer ban," *The Mercury*, 1.

18. Michael Moyer, letter to the editor, *The Mercury*, September 5, 1990, 6.

19. Ann Bradley, "Christian activists set their sights on school board seats," *Education Week*, October 7, 1992, 1, 16.

20. The National Association of Christian Educators/Citizens for Excellence in Education (CEE) was located in Costa Mesa, California. Robert Simonds, president of the organization, stated in the December, 1991, *President's Report* that the organization had a national network of 868 chapters. In 2006, he claimed that CEE had more than 1680 chapters representing more than 350,000 active parents.

21. "Tremendous victory in school board race," *Education Newsline*, September/October, 1992 (Costa Mesa, CA: National Association of Christian Educators/Citizens for Excellence in Education), 1–4.

22. Ibid.

23. Robert Simonds, *President's Report* (Costa Mesa, CA: National Association of Christian Educators/Citizens for Excellence in Education, December, 1991).

24. Ernest Hemingway, *The Old Man and the Sea* (New York: Macmillan Publishing, 1952), 62.

25. Maxine Greene, *Landscapes for Learning* (New York: Teachers College Press, 1978), 166.

26. Ibid.

27. Greene, *Variations*, 116.

28. Greene, *Landscapes*, 166.

29. Raymond Horn, "Differing perspectives on the magic of dialogue: Implications for scholar-practitioner leader," *Scholar Practitioner Quarterly*, vol. 1, no. 2 (2002), 84.

30. Ibid., 100.

31. Alexander Sidorkin, *Beyond Discourse: Education, the Self, and Dialogue* (Albany: State University of New York Press, 1999), 4.

32. Ibid., 14.

33. Ibid., 18.

Chapter 4

Combating a Neo-Nazi Hate Group

Sieg Heil to the Aryan race and to those who are willing to fight and die for it!¹

As with the phoenix who is reborn in fire, so the Pottstown S.S. rises from the ashes left behind by their fore bearers to create a new and better elite force to serve the Aryan cause.²
—Neo-Nazi Recruitment Flyer

HATED FROM NEO-NAZIS IN POTTSTOWN, PENNSYLVANIA

A Fearsome Neo-Nazi Recruitment Flyer

This chapter's opening quotations are taken from a neo-Nazi recruitment flyer that was distributed throughout the Owen J. Roberts school district in early April 1994. The flyer called for a student boycott on May 6 to commemorate the anniversary death of Heinrich Himmler. Himmler has become a glorified Nazi god from the past. His ruthlessness enabled him to rise quickly among the Nazi elite to become second-in-command behind only Hitler himself. At forty-four years of age, his star collapsed leaving a giant black hole of notoriety that is being fathomed by neo-Nazis today.

Himmler committed suicide on May 23, 1945, by biting into a concealed cyanide tablet after being captured by British forces. As *Reichsführer* to Adolf Hitler, he created and was head of the dreaded *Schutz Staffel* (SS) forces. The SS were organized into three separate branches: the *Allgemeine* SS who were responsible for enforcing Nazi racist laws; the *Waffen* SS who were part of the military; and the *Totenkopfverbände* SS who ran the concentration and extermination camps.

SS uniforms and insignia separated them from other police and military forces. Most recognizable were the twin lightning bolts whose origins have been traced to the pre-Roman runic alphabet representing the "s" sound.[3] These bolts caused numbing fear and horror when enslaved populations or prisoners encountered soldiers wearing them. An example was provided by Joseph (Joe) Brozozowski who was the enslaved Polish boy that we met in chapter 2.

Joe described an episode when a prisoner complained about the food. The woman who was feeding him reported his complaint to the German police. An SS officer was dispatched to see the prisoner. The officer beat the prisoner to death on the spot.[4] It is this dread-filled notoriety of the SS bolts that has, according to the Anti-Defamation League (ADL), caused many neo-Nazis and White supremacists to adopt them as part of pseudo-military uniforms or tattoos.[5]

The recruitment flyer handed out to high school students has the SS bolts in the upper right-hand corner. In the opposite corner is a drawing of a presumably White male in pseudo-military uniform. Centered at the top is the name "Himmler" beneath which are his birth and death dates (October 7, 1900 to May 23, 1945). Next to this is a call for a school-wide boycott on May 1, 1994, to honor Himmler's death day. Beneath the call for a boycott is the address of the Pottstown *Schutz Staffel* (Pottstown Schutz Staffel, Headquarters, P.O. Box 1439, Pottstown, Pa, 19464). Filling at least two-thirds of the flyer in the center is a crude drawing of Himmler flanked by Nazi banners complete with *Swastikas*.[6]

A statement on the back of the flyer lays out the purpose of Pottstown SS:

> The P.S.S. is an organization modeled after the original S.S. of Nazi Germany which was head [*sic*] by Heinrich Himmler. The P.S.S was founded by [name deleted by author] and [name deleted by author] in 1994. [name deleted by author] and [name deleted by author] decided to create this organization in the hopes that it will help to further the Aryan cause left to us by our predecessor Führer Adolf Hitler.
>
> It was he and Himmler who gave these men the ambition, courage and fervor to create their own organization. Their goal is to make the P.S.S. as powerful and as highly regarded as the first S.S. They hope that it will also give Aryan men who truly believe in their race the opportunity to fight to keep their race safe and strong even if it means their deaths in the process.[7]

One sentence, in particular, seems to jump off the flyer. It should alarm us today as much as it did those who read it nearly thirty years ago: "[Founders of the P.S.S.] decided to create this organization in the hopes that it will help to further the Aryan cause left to us by our predecessor Führer Adolf

Hitler."[8] The philosophy of a superior race, the Aryan race, is forcefully laid out by Hitler in his *Mein Kamph* (My Struggle) which he began writing in 1924 while serving time in Landsberg prison for an attempt to overthrow the German government.

Mein Kampf became a blueprint for later Nazi actions regarding racial superiority and the extermination of inferior races, especially Jews. In the darkest terms, this is the foundation upon which hatred between races is built. Here are some of Hitler's own words from *Mein Kampf*:

> What we see before us of human culture today, the results of art, science, and techniques, is almost exclusively the creative product of the Aryan. . . . The "Aryan" succeeds in pushing his way onward and upward by conquering lesser people and using them as "helping forces" (slaves).[9]

No doubt left to the imagination—the flyer is from a White supremacist neo-Nazi group. This was not child's play—it was deadly serious. The recruitment and boycott attempts became a teachable moment that united a community in affirmation of its anti-Nazi/anti-racist values. The action took place in a generally placid school district located approximately forty miles from Philadelphia.

Neo-Nazi Confrontation in a Peaceful School District

The Owen J. Roberts School District covers approximately 108 square miles in bucolic northern Chester County, Pennsylvania. This is a prosperous area and one of the fastest-growing in the region. It is known for pastoral settings of open space and rolling countryside. Drive thirty minutes to the south and you are in some of Philadelphia's emerging affluent suburbs. The same distance to the east is historic Valley Forge. To the west is Amish country where the nineteenth-century sounds of horses' hooves remind us of a peaceful past era. To the north, approaching the Lehigh Valley, the landscape looks similarly peaceful.

Traveling north, however, can also take you to one of the hotbeds of White supremacy. In the 1990s, racial hatred was openly evident on a compound dedicated to the training of neo-Nazis. In April 1994, Mark Thomas's compound near *Seisholtzville* in Berks County was anything but peaceful. It was here that Thomas hosted a weekend Hitler Youth Festival attended by approximately 200 neo-Nazis and other White supremacists.[10] The Pottstown SS was formed from this group and inspiration for the distribution of recruitment flyers and the proposed boycott came from this rally.

The peaceful quiet that often accompanies the warming of a mid-April morning was broken harshly when several alarmed high school students arrived at school with the flyers. In this dramatic way, one of a school district's most dreaded nightmares—a community upheaval fed by rampant rumors and fears of violence against students—became a reality.

Anxious Questions Abounded

The switchboard lit up as news of the flyers and the impending boycott quickly spread throughout the district. Teachers were looking for direction on what to tell their students. Central office administrators asked them to remain calm and quickly assured them through emails and personal school visits that district security plans would ensure the safety of students and staff members. These same administrators also knew that even the best plans are not always successful.

Calls from staff members were followed by other frantic parents and citizens. They wanted to know answers to a myriad of questions. What did the school administration know about the neo-Nazi group that was distributing the flyers? How do hate groups recruit members? Was this threat real and what could be expected in the way of violence? Would classes be canceled? If schools remained open, how could administrators and teachers guarantee the safety of all students? What could the community do to keep groups such as this from disrupting its schools?

Policies were in place to deal with immediate safety and security concerns. These were not sufficient, however, to answer the questions coming from all sides. The district did not have a strategy to keep a hate group from establishing a lasting presence in the school community. There were approximately two weeks before the boycott. This provided time to develop a crisis blueprint to deal with the impending crisis.

A Crisis Blueprint

The day after the flyers appeared, the district's leadership team discussed ways of dealing with the imminent crisis. First and foremost, it reviewed the district's security arrangements. This was followed by launching a thorough communication plan to keep all constituencies fully informed of actions in dealing with the emergency.

The communications plan included announcements, mailings, and public media information provided to students, parents, religious leaders, government officials, and general community members. These are prudent measures usually taken in dealing with such situations. District teachers and administrators wanted to do more. They recognized the emergency as a significant opportunity to lead the district in confronting raw hatred and bigotry—indeed a teachable moment. With this end in mind, they contacted the Pennsylvania Human Relations Commission for advice.

As chance would have it, one of the commission's experts on intolerance, Ann Van Dyke, was scheduled to come to the school district the same week that the flyers appeared. She was scheduled to give a culminating presentation to the high school faculty who were engaged in a series of dialogue sessions regarding human rights issues. The focus for these sessions was a study of the holocaust as there was interest in developing interdisciplinary studies on this topic. These sessions were planned by a highly respected high school teacher along with the building principal and district superintendent.

Accompanied by a human rights specialist from the Pennsylvania State Police, Major Garcia, Van Dyke began the high school dialogue session by informing teachers that Pennsylvania led the nation that year with forty-four active hate groups. She informed the teachers that the neo-Nazi organization known as the Pottstown SS was unknown to her. It appeared to be a relatively small organization.

Large or small was not the issue. She explained that violence can come in any size and then described the serious problems that a nearby school district was having in confronting the Keystone Knights, a local affiliate of the Ku Klux Klan. Distressed by this information, teachers asked the big question— how does a school district combat this hatred and keep such groups from establishing themselves in a community?

Van Dyke began to answer the question by leading the group through an insightful two-page newsletter entitled "How Hate Groups Recruit Our Young People" prepared by Floyd Cochran, a former propaganda minister of a White supremacist group known as Church of Jesus Christ Christian/Aryan Nations. Cochran had been involved in various racist movements for more than twenty years and left the Church of Jesus Christ Christian/Aryan Nations only after his son was born with a cleft palate and his superiors told him that he was now considered racially inferior. Angered, he did an about-face and began to use his inside knowledge of hate group's operations to inform young people across the country of their dangers.

In his newsletter, prepared for the Montana Office of Public Instruction, Cochran addressed the basic human need of belonging. He wrote that upon entering the movement he felt as if he was part of not only of a family but also of a movement that was important and larger than he was. He indicated that many young racists come from dysfunctional families. Most are alienated from school. They look elsewhere to fulfill their need to belong. He wrote that hate groups are there, waiting for them.[11]

After reviewing Floyd Cochran's newsletter, Ann Van Dyke described actions that had proven successful in other communities which had encountered hate groups. She referenced several points from a document of hers entitled "So Now What Do You Do?" Her advice included:

- forming a unity coalition and defining the community as one that honors unity, tolerance, and diversity;
- redirecting energy and attention to positive community events that build harmony among citizens;
- ensuring that the school district has a multicultural curriculum and cultural awareness training for all staff members;
- establishing an ongoing adult education program that includes religious, civic, and other community groups; and
- listening to youth and including them in planning various school and community activities.[12]

Several of her points formed the blueprint for actions led by the district's high school teachers.

Teachers Lead the Way in Avoiding a Crisis

A series of dialogue sessions throughout the district had become the heart of a professional development program designed to aid teachers in becoming both the chief architects as well as implementers of the district's curriculum. A majority of the high school teachers were involved in dialogue sessions during the 1993–1994 school year that were aimed at developing an interdisciplinary curriculum based on encounters with intolerance.

Special focus was on the Holocaust. Some of the materials for these sessions were Stanley Elkin's book *Slavery*, Elie Wiesel's *The Night Trilogy*, and Steven Spielberg's movie *Schindler's List*. In addition to dialogue sessions held at the high school, participants visited the holocaust museum in Washington.

As a result of these dialogue sessions, many teachers felt an increased sensitivity toward human rights issues. They decided to take the lead in mobilizing teachers throughout the district. They were the ones who planned a series of activities to take place on the day of the proposed boycott. These included developing lessons on hate-group dynamics and human rights issues. These were designed for high and middle school students as both were the immediate focus of the recruitment and the boycott efforts.

Teachers also organized a no-putdown-day complete with suggested activities and buttons for all K-12 staff and students. These were especially valuable for elementary students. It opened the way to various discussions that dealt with intolerance and the need to be respectful of individual differences. Primary students, for example, talked about different ways to avoid conflicts in classrooms, on playgrounds, and in neighborhood settings. The neo-Nazis had provided a powerful teachable moment that led to substantive discussions that might otherwise not have happened.

Teacher leadership was crucial in planning these activities and proved to be important in soothing community uneasiness. Most teachers were well known and respected by the majority of parents. They became trusted communicators. Their presence along with administrators and police outside of their schools on the morning of the boycott proved to be a deciding factor in calming fears and quelling the boycott.

For all practical purposes, the boycott fizzled. Attendance at the schools was nearly normal with a slight dip recorded at the high school. Many students later provided an explanation for this when they admitted the boycott gave them a great opportunity to skip school on a sunny spring day. Many also made it clear their absence was not intended as a show of support for the neo-Nazis.

Once the initial crisis passed without incident, it became possible for teachers, administrators, school board members, and students to begin to implement some of the long-range plans based on the points shared by Ann Van Dyke at the high school dialogue session.

Building for the Future

Ann Van Dyke gave two key pointers to keep hate groups from establishing a foothold in a community:

- form a unity coalition and define your community as one that honors unity, tolerance, and diversity; and
- redirect energy and attention to positive community events that build harmony among citizens.

Forming a unity coalition became a central focus, and more than 150 parents, students, and community representatives attended a meeting that was designed to form one. At the meeting, teachers and administrators led small-group discussions that focused on the information regarding hate-group dynamics provided by the Pennsylvania Human Rights Commission. Attendance remained strong at several other sessions that were held throughout that year.

It is not easy to measure the long-term effects that this neo-Nazi threat had on this school community. There were no pre or posttests, no statistics to validate the success or failure of actions taken, no benchmarks or percentages to measure progress. This may be troubling in a society that increasingly relies upon statistics to prove the success of educational initiatives. What did emerge was a greater awareness of hate groups and their attempts to strike out both at schools and society in general.

The neo-Nazi confrontation revealed a set of positive social values within the community. One example was the formation of an educational foundation dedicated to human rights issues. The formation of the foundation demonstrated an awareness regarding the potential danger of hate groups.

Change and the Establishment of an Education Foundation

The dynamics of change present a constant dialectic between conservative forces for stability (thesis) and forces that question and probe the values and actions of the thesis (antithesis). Eventually, this dialectic of moving forces resolves itself and becomes stable (synthesis). Over time, the synthesis can become a new thesis, another antithesis arises, and eventually a new synthesis emerges. The process continues unless slowed by institutionalization of the synthesis. The degree of slowing depends on the strength of the institutionalization (figure 4.1).

The establishment of organized religions provides good examples. Let us consider Christianity. Think of the Jewish religion and culture around 33 BC as the thesis. Jesus of Nazareth's ministry and proclamation as the long-awaited Messiah can be seen as the antithesis. Early Christianity became a new synthesis which within the first two centuries became highly institutionalized. The dynamic forces of the early church became almost frozen and a formidable thesis. Although there have been many challenges and changes to this institutionalization—for example, the Reformation and Vatican II—it has remained remarkably stable for more than 2,000 years.

The confrontation with the neo-Nazis in the Owen J. Roberts school district is a good example of similar forces at work. The peaceful community (thesis) was challenged by the forces of the neo-Nazis (antithesis). In the process, a

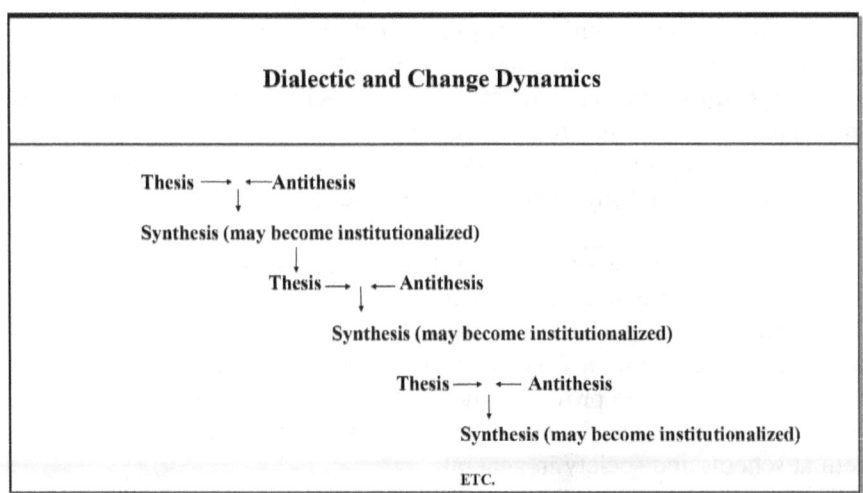

Figure 4.1 **Dialectic and Change Dynamics.** *Source:* Author Created.

defined set of community values emerged (synthesis). In this instance, the community determined that the values of the neo-Nazis were not the ones that they wanted to be their own. Now the question that arose—can this new synthesis be institutionalized? This was the thinking behind the establishment of the Owen J. Roberts Educational Foundation.

The Owen J. Roberts Education Foundation, complete with bylaws and a board of directors representing a cross section of the community, became a reality within a few months of the proposed neo-Nazi boycott. Its first major function was to plan an event designed to bring together citizens, parents, and students to honor the district's namesake, Owen J. Roberts.

As a former justice of the U.S. Supreme Court, Owen J. Roberts often supported important human rights issues such as opposition to the relocation of Japanese Americans during World War II. Although Roberts was a former resident of the community and a member of the board of education that had voted to unify seven separate school districts into one, many people did not know about his important role on human rights issues.

For this reason, the Owen J. Roberts Education Foundation Board decided to place its initial focus on providing a greater knowledge of his life and significant activities. The date for a commemoration of Roberts's life was purposefully chosen to coincide with the first anniversary of the proposed neo-Nazi boycott.

More than 700 parents and community members attended a Sunday afternoon program that memorialized Owen J. Roberts through the screening of a video of historical events regarding his life that was produced by school district personnel. This event triggered a fundraising campaign that netted more than 20,000 dollars for the foundation during its first year. The money established annual human rights seminars for students, teachers, and community members to coincide with the anniversary date of the boycott. The first featured speaker was Floyd Cochran, the former member of the Church of Jesus Christ Christian/Aryan Nations.

Floyd Cochran's powerful lessons to middle and high school students during the day were a prelude to his evening presentation to more than 500 citizens. Special security guards were needed as his life had been threatened by members of his former Aryan Nations hate group. He stunned listeners as he described his role in recruitment activities and the violent acts he committed against minorities. Cochran's work on the advisory board of the Pennsylvania Alliance for Democracy as well as the education staff of the Liberty Museum & Education Center in Philadelphia is known by hundreds who have seen evidence of his advocacy for important human rights causes.

The Owen J. Roberts education foundation has continued to this day as a vibrant organization with its original mission broadened. As stated on the Foundation's Web page: "The Owen J. Roberts Education Foundation is a

501(c)(3)charity that operates independently from the district and is dedicated to encouraging community-wide participation and philanthropy in order to support educational innovation and the Mission of the OJRSD."[13]

The picture above these words on the Foundation's website (https://ojref.org/) captures the human rights essence that underpinned the Foundation's origins. It shows a moment with a young man in the near-center of seven elementary-aged children of mixed races and gender. They are all engaged on iPads in front of a bank of colorful books—a powerful image, indeed.

HATE GROUPS FOUND IN ALL PARTS OF THE UNITED STATES

The Southern Poverty Law Center (SPLC) is a remarkably vibrant organization that tracks and confronts the hate groups in the United States. It also provides a rich array of resources and materials for educators on ways to combat hatred on multiple levels. As stated on its website: "The SPLC was founded in 1971 to ensure that the promise of the civil rights movement became a reality for all."[14] The promise referenced above was made a reality in the Civil Rights Act of 1964 and the Voting Rights Act of 1965.

These sweeping actions by Congress were necessitated when the guarantees of full citizenship and voting rights made to former slaves in the 13th, 14th, and 15th Amendments to the Constitution became hollow phrases because of the rise of Jim Crow and White/Black segregation. The SPLC's founder, Morris Dees, is the son of an Alabama farmer who witnessed firsthand the destructive effects of segregation and racial hatred. He eventually sold his book publishing business and focused his career on being a civil rights lawyer.[15]

According to the Southern Poverty Law Center, 838 active hate groups operated in the United States in 2020.[16] As previously stated in chapter 2, the SPLC defines a hate group as "an organization or collection of individuals that—based on its official statements or principles, the statements of its leaders, or its activities—has beliefs or practices that attack or malign an entire class of people, typically for their immutable characteristics."[17] What is remarkable is the depth of information assembled by the SPLC regarding various hate groups in the United States.

Here are some examples of hate-group information available from the SPLC:

- Hate groups listed by ideology. It can be accessed at: https://www.splcenter.org/fighting-hate/extremist-files/ideology

- An interactive hate map showing the most prominent hate groups located in each state. It can be accessed at https://www.splcenter.org/hate-map.

After spending some time on these and other SPLC sites, the depth and breadth of hate groups become shockingly evident. Educators at all levels need to have a basic awareness of these groups if they are going to prepare themselves, their students, and communities for a possible confrontation such as that which occurred in the Owner J. Roberts school district. In addition to SPLC, other resources that can be helpful in preparing for and/or confronting hate groups are as follows:

- The Anti-Defamation League provides antibias curricula resources and interactive training programs for educators (www.adl.org).
- The Council on American-Islamic Relations offers a series of guides to explain Muslim religious practices to educators (www.caor.com).
- The Pennsylvania Human Relations Commission educates both educators and students on civil rights (phrc.pa.gov).
- The United Nations Human Rights Council offers publications and resources supporting human rights education (www.ohchr.org/ED/PublicationsResources/Pages/TrainingEducation.aspx).
- BaFa' BaFa' offers an interactive simulation that is designed to provide diversity training for educators (https://www.simulationtrainingsystems.com).

SUMMARY: LESSONS LEARNED

There are many lessons in this chapter for educators combating hatred. These include:

- educators at all levels, particularly those in leadership positions, need to be aware of hate groups that may be operating in their area;
- taking all threats seriously—they are not child's play;
- having clear policies in place on ways to deal with hate groups and hate-group threats;
- communicating clearly, completely, often on various platforms, and to a wide range of constituents regarding hate groups and threats;
- utilizing various state and national resources and organizations that have experience in dealing with hate groups;
- using crises as teachable moments to create communities of learners; and
- understanding the dynamics of change and aiming to institutionalize positive changes that come from teachable moments created by crises.

In his description of Aryan Nation recruitment tactics, Floyd Cochran said that the most vulnerable targets were youth who were alienated from their schools. Such alienation has led to numerous violent school tragedies over the past few years. The next chapter, "Transformational Educators Combating Student Alienation," will consider student alienation from both philosophical and practical perspectives.

NOTES

1. Emmanuel Clary, "Himmler Flyer," distributed throughout Owen J. Roberts School District, April 1994.
2. Ibid.
3. SS Bolts, ADL (Anti-Defamation League), https://www.adl.org/education/references/hate-symbols/ss-bolts (accessed August 18, 2021).
4. The information regarding Joseph Brzozowski comes from various conversations and interviews with Terrance Furin from August 2019 to September 2021.
5. Ibid., SS Bolts.
6. Neo-Nazi recruitment flyer, April, 1994. A copy is in the possession of the author.
7. Ibid.
8. Ibid.
9. Adolf Hitler, *Mein Kampf* (Boston: Houghton Mifflin, 1939), 397, https://archive.org/stream/meinkampf035176mbp/meinkampf035176mbp_djvu.txt (accessed August 22, 2021).
10. Mark Schneider, "Triple murder causes alarm about hate groups' growth," *New York Times*, March 6, 1995, http://query.nytimes.com/gst/fullpage.html?res=990CE5D91238F935A35750C0A963958260&sec=&spon=&pagewanted=all (accessed January 23, 2018).
11. Floyd Cochran, "How hate groups recruit our young people," *Newsletter of the Montana Office of Public Instruction*, November/December 1992.
12. Ann Van Dyke, "So Now What Do You do?" Pennsylvania Human Relations Council, distributed to Owen J. Roberts high school dialogue group, April 26, 1994.
13. "Welcome to the Owen J. Roberts Educational Foundation," https://ojref.org/ (accessed August 19, 2021).
14. "Our History," Southern Poverty Law Center, https://www.splcenter.org/about-us/our-history (accessed August 23, 2021).
15. Ibid.
16. "Hate groups across the united states," Southern Poverty Law Center, https://www.splcenter.org/hate-map (accessed August 22, 2021).
17. Southern Poverty Law Center definition of a hate group, https://www.splcenter.org/20200318/frequently-asked-questions-about-hate-groups#hate%20group (accessed July 22, 2021).

Chapter 5

Transformational Educators Combating Student Alienation

"Massacre at columbine high, bloodbath leaves 15 dead, 28 hurt,"[1]
—*Denver Post*, April 21, 1999.

"'A horrific, horrific day': At least 17 killed in Florida school shooting,"[2]
—*The Washington Post*, February 15, 2018.

"Aztec High School shooting: 2 slain students identified,"[3]
—*CNN*, December 8, 2017.

"There have been 14 school shootings this year, 73 since 2018,"[4]
—*Education Week*, September 2, 2021

STUDENTS AS KILLERS

The first three examples quoted above are of multiple school shootings by students which have occurred in the United States in recent years. The first tells of the horrendous 1999 Columbine massacre which cast a national spotlight on alienated students striking back at their classmates. The second deals with the infamous school shooting at Parkland, Florida's Marjory Stoneman Douglas High School where another alienated student brutally used an assault rifle to mow down students at his former high school.

The third example is of yet another vicious shooting where a former student of Aztec High School in Aztec, New Mexico, entered the school and killed two students who were barricaded inside an office area. The final quotation is a 2021 update of school shootings from *Education Week*, a highly respected newspaper for educators. In 2018 *Education Week*'s journalists began tracking school shootings that resulted in injuries or deaths. There is a downward trend in 2020–2021 which can be explained by the fact that most students were not physically present in school buildings during the COVID-19 pandemic.

While these may seem like extreme examples, most schools have many alienated students. Some are isolated individuals. Others cluster together in groups that go by various names. The disappointment, resentment, and revulsion that many of them feel toward their schools usually remain bottled up. Sometimes, as these headlines proclaim, alienation turns into hatred that ends in violence. Such acts expose serious flaws both in our society and the educational system that nourishes it.

The stories accompanying these headlines present facts and narratives that capture the depths of these calamities. They suggest that cultural or social factors may have contributed to the apparent dysfunction of the killers. What they do not do is probe in any substantive way the possibility that one of the major contributing factors may be the schools themselves.

There are many inherent imperfections in the high-stakes testing philosophy that has dominated our schools for the past several years. Beginning in the 1980s, this movement reached a climax with the No Child Left Behind Act of 2001 and continues today with national and state tests dictated by federal Common Core standards. Preparation for high-stakes testing often eliminates or reduces subjects other than reading/language arts and math from the curriculum. Pressure on students is often extreme.

As one fifth-grade Pennsylvania student reported to her principal, when asked what her dream for the school year was, she responded "I hope that I can just become proficient (average) this year"[5] It has ironically left many not only behind but also estranged by an educational system that was supposed to lead them into full citizenship as members of our democratic society.

This chapter briefly examines some roots of the high-stakes testing philosophy that dominates American education today. It presents a contrasting child-centered philosophy and examples from elementary, middle, and high schools where teachers and educational leaders made a significant difference in alleviating some of the causes of student alienation.

MODERNITY, EFFICIENCY, AND NO CHILD LEFT BEHIND

The basic tenets of the No Child Left Behind Act and the state tests dictated by the federal Common Core standards are rooted in the modern era of the twentieth century. Frederick W. Taylor's efficiency movement imposed a high degree of standardization on many aspects of American life including education. It was this movement that introduced us to the idea that standards and their assessments should be set by specialists rather than classroom teachers and school leaders. A basic organizational chart typical of most school districts resembles a top-down administrative structure such as that seen in figure 5.1.

In this model, it is assumed that power flows from top to bottom. Students and parents seldom appear on such charts. If teachers are included, they are usually at the bottom where they receive directives from above. A similar organizational chart can be seen in a satire of the efficiency movement created by Charlie Chaplin in his classic 1936 movie *Modern Times*.

Modern Times

Charlie Chaplin wrote, directed, and starred in *Modern Times*—a film that presents a stinging indictment of an assembly line where the efficiency movement has turned the workers into automatons trapped by the forces of a technological society gone awry. Chaplin is a helpless individual deeply affected

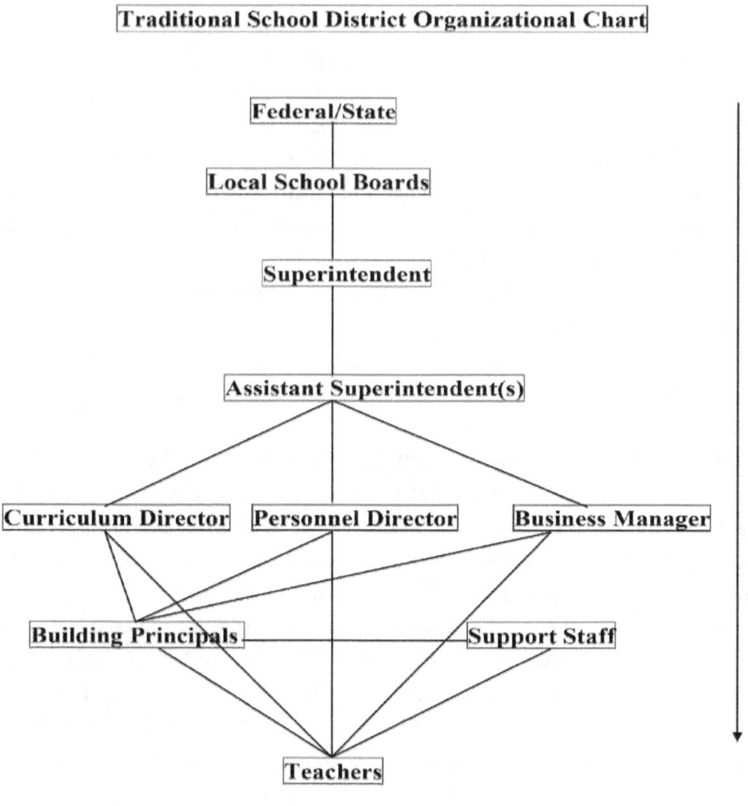

Traditional School District Organizational Chart

Federal/State
│
Local School Boards
│
Superintendent
│
Assistant Superintendent(s)
╱   │   ╲
Curriculum Director   Personnel Director   Business Manager

Building Principals ──── Support Staff

Teachers

Figure 5.1 Traditional School District Organizational Chart. *Source*: Author Created.

by the actions of a heartless bureaucracy whose only concern is bottom-line profits.

His job as a worker on an assembly line at the Electro Steel Company is to tighten bolts on some imaginary product. He does this until he becomes dazed from the monotonous repetition and is granted permission to punch out on the time clock in order to take a break. While in the restroom he lights a cigarette and begins to unwind. The relaxation is short-lived as the corporate boss suddenly appears on a wall-sized TV monitor (this in 1936) and orders him back to work.

The boss controls all aspects of the company's operations while at ease in his comfortable office. He lackadaisically reads comics from a newspaper, arranges pieces of a puzzle, and occasionally gives orders to his secretary. His main function appears to be observing the efficiency of all assembly line jobs. Periodically he orders the line supervisor to speed up Charlie's line. This causes Charlie to fall behind. Fellow workers become angry. He eventually cracks under the strain, falls into a trance-like state, and becomes caught between phantasmagorical motorized gears.[6]

The issues of power and control portrayed in these scenes are enormous. Workers had no voice in decisions affecting the quality of their products or other aspects of their jobs. Efficiency experts, pictured in one scene attempting to modernize the lunch break through a mechanical feeding machine, made decisions which were enforced by commanding authorities. The workers had no stake in the organization other than receiving their paychecks. In most respects, they were captives of a system wherein they were isolated and controlled by a powerful force they seldom saw.

In many respects, their factory resembled the panopticon prisons described by the French philosopher Michel Foucault in his book *Discipline and Punish* (New York: Vintage Books, 1979). In such a prison inmates were controlled by a powerful central tower where a faceless power unknown to them directed all aspects of their lives.

Charlie's factory differed from a panopticon prison in one major aspect. The prison existed strictly to control inmates. The factory controlled workers in order to manufacture products. The ends of the prison became the means of the factory. In such an environment the workers were invested in the finished product only as far as their specific task was concerned.

It is assumed from the movie that each assembly line added small contributions until the product was completed. At this point in the manufacturing process, it is usual for trained inspectors to sort, examine, and measure the products. If within established tolerances, they are sent out into the world. If not, they are recycled or discarded. Comparisons can be readily made between an assembly line process, such as the one created on film by Charlie Chaplin, and many American schools today.

Students as Products

The No Child Left Behind Act (NCLB) of 2001 and subsequent state tests and standards, such as the federal Common Core, treat students as products which are regularly sorted, examined, and measured through a system of high-stakes tests. Though they may differ from state to state, their purpose is the same—assess students regularly to determine if they, the teacher, and the school have made yearly progress. The testing pressure on students is enormous. Failure to meet test standards can mean that students will be recycled through after-school or summertime remediation programs. Many of these students, especially when reaching high school, will be discarded altogether.

The pressure on teachers and building principals, particularly at the elementary level, is also huge. They know that if their class or building does not reach targeted annual goals they stand the risk of being transferred or losing their jobs.[7] In this high anxiety environment, they often ignore the mandated curriculum and focus on the subjects that will be tested—reading, language arts, and math. The tests dictate the curriculum.

One example of this deference to high-stakes tests is seen in Philadelphia where thirteen fifth- and sixth-grade teachers received an email from an assistant principal instructing them to stop teaching the state-mandated social studies curriculum from December through April. The time scheduled for social studies was to be used for math instead. Math was considered of vital importance because of the impending exams in April. Social studies was not a subject tested for annual progress.[8] Another example is found in a suburban Philadelphia school district where a superintendent ordered principals to stop teaching elementary science and social studies altogether and concentrate instead on reading, language arts, and math.[9]

As with the workers on the assembly line in Charlie's factory, mandated tests focus on narrow tasks. There is an assumption that somehow, someplace, someone else is responsible for the final product. Social studies, a subject that includes topics concerned with citizenship preparation, will only be measured later by the quality of a person's participation in a democratic society. Sadly, many will not participate at all.

A common philosophy regarding power relationships and the value of individuals unites the assembly line factory depicted by Chaplin and a school driven by high-stakes tests. It is found in John Locke's seventeenth-century views of a child at birth.

John Locke's "White Paper"

John Locke was an immensely significant seventeenth-century philosopher who greatly influenced the formation of our nation. His *Second Treatise of*

Government was read widely by many of the founding fathers. His basic concepts regarding the intrinsic rights of individuals versus the authority of a monarchy inspired Thomas Jefferson and others to write the Declaration of Independence. In this same treatise, Locke presents arguments for the sanctity of private property, a limitation on the authority of central government, and a separation of power between legislative and executive functions.

Locke was also an educational philosopher. His ideas concerning the nature of a child at birth are as influential in American culture today as are his political thoughts. He believed that a child at birth was "white paper, void of all characters, without any ideas."[10] This *tabula rasa* or blank slate philosophy places vast authority and responsibility for a person's education in the hands of parents and teachers. Inherent in such authority and responsibility is the power to control the individual until they reach a majority age, identified by Locke in *The Second Treatise* as twenty-one.

Locke's white-paper philosophy denies the innate qualities of a child at birth. If the opposite is true—if a child at birth has intrinsic capacities, passions, and talents—then the notion of total control by those in authority needs to be modified. The implications of this change for education are enormous. They place the student in the center rather than at the bottom of a system's organizational chart.

AN ALTERNATIVE PHILOSOPHY

Placing the Student in the Center

As pictured previously, an organizational chart dominated by efficiency concerns and based upon a *tabula rasa* philosophy of a child at birthplaces the student at the bottom. An alternative philosophy, one that places the child at the center of the educational process, resembles a series of circles as shown in figure 5.2.

Placing the student at the center of the process dramatically shifts relationships. This presents a different way of considering the power that flows both from students and to students. The importance of considering the unique gifts that students bring to their educational experience is emphasized in this visualization. An effective way of thinking about the importance of each position relative to the daily education of a student is to consider the amount of intended education that takes place if each individual on the chart is unexpectedly absent from school.

If the student is absent, little designated education will take place. If the teacher is absent, there may be some education provided there is a skilled substitute. If a support staff member (secretary, aide, bus driver, custodian, cafeteria worker) misses a day, the class will continue to function fairly normally.

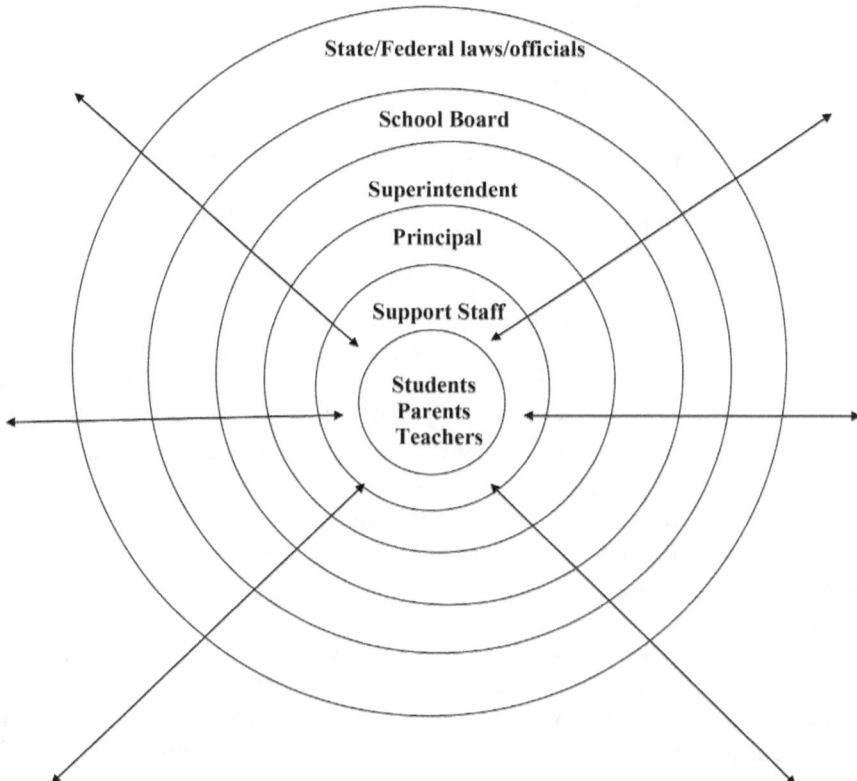

Figure 5.2 Student at the Center of the Organizational Structure for Education.
Source: Author Created.

If the principal is absent, few will notice. If the superintendent or another central office staff member misses a day, hardly anyone will notice. School board members, as well as state and federal officials, seldom visit schools during the day and are not usually well known by teachers and students.

The educational philosophy supporting placing the child in the center of the educational hierarchy comes from another famous political theorist who is also prominent as an educational philosopher—Jean Jacques Rousseau.

Jean Jacques Rousseau and a "Cathedral Within"

Jean Jacques Rousseau is one of France's revolutionary heroes. His stinging antiestablishment works made him a venerated philosopher of the 1789 revolution. Consider one example: he begins Book One of *On the Social Contract* with words that have inspired not only French but other revolutionaries as well—"Man is born free and everywhere he is in chains."[11]

Rousseau's views on education are similarly radical and differ dramatically from Locke's *tabula rasa*. His *Discourse on the Arts and Sciences*, written in 1750, was the winning entry to an essay contest question regarding whether the advancement of the arts and sciences had improved morals. He answered strongly that it had not. This essay argued in effect that education can corrupt the beauty of an individual at birth. He wrote in his book on education, *Emile*, that "everything is good as it leaves the hands of the Author of things; everything degenerates in the hands of man."[12]

An effective metaphor that captures Rousseau's view of a child at birth is provided by Norman Cousins, the former editor of the *Saturday Review* magazine. Cousins interviewed many of the world's most influential people and often asked them to describe the most important thing they had learned in their lifetime. One of these was the 1952 Nobel Peace Prize recipient, Albert Schweitzer. Talented as a writer, musician, scientist, and doctor, he could have lived a comfortable life. He chose a different path and established medical clinics where none existed in the tropics of Africa.

Cousins traveled far into a jungle to interview Schweitzer and during a meal one evening asked this question. Schweitzer said that he would have to think about his response and would have an answer the following day. The next morning Cousins awoke to find that Schweitzer had gone into a neighboring village to help deliver a baby. After his return that evening, Schweitzer told Cousins he had thought about the question throughout the day and saw his answer in the newborn infant. He believed that the most important thing he had learned in his lifetime was that each person contains a "cathedral within."[13]

Schweitzer's metaphor, captured by Cousins, is of a vast, beautiful, sacred newborn. It is consistent with Rousseau's philosophy and creates a tense dialectic with John Locke's white-paper image. It is this dialectic that America's most famous educational philosopher, John Dewey, attempted to resolve through his theories that consistently place the child in the center of the educational process.

John Dewey and the Significance of Placing the Child in the Center

John Dewey wrestled with Locke and Rousseau's educational theories and attempted to resolve them.[14] In doing so, he leaned more toward Rousseau's view and placed the child in the center of the educational process. This was a radical departure in American education when it was presented more than 120 years ago. It continues to create significant tensions as it confronts the dominant top-down, child-control theory, evident in the high-stakes testing movement that drives American education today. The following quotation from Dewey's *The Child and the Curriculum* captures the heart of Dewey's philosophy:

> The child is the starting-point, the center, and the end. His development, his growth, is the ideal. It alone furnishes the standard. To the growth of the child all studies are subservient; they are instruments valued as they serve the needs of growth. Personality, character, is more than subject-matter. Not knowledge or information, but self-realization, is the goal. To possess all the world of knowledge and lose one's own self is as awful a fate in education as in religion. Moreover, subject-matter never can be got into the child from without. Learning is active. It involves reaching out of the mind. It involves organic assimilation starting from within.[15]

The progressive philosophy summarized by this quotation challenges the very basis of an educational system that imposes a curriculum dictated by high-stakes tests upon students. It recognizes that true learning starts from within each individual and can lead to unique self-actualization. Dewey does not stop here. He believed further that the individual is situated within a democratic social context and that developing values of social worth is a critical component of each student's education.[16]

The significance of these beliefs cannot be overemphasized. It is in this philosophy that the possibilities of confronting hatred which often grow out of student alienation lie. Many school leaders on all levels—principals, teachers, superintendents—have applied the core aspects of Dewey's philosophy in specific situations and have made a difference in student's lives.

THEORY TO PRACTICE: CONFRONTING ALIENATION BEFORE IT TURNS INTO HATRED OR VIOLENCE

Meade Elementary School

Located on North 18th Street, General George C. Meade Elementary School is in one of the most economically disadvantaged areas of Philadelphia. From a distance, Meade is an imposing structure. The school was built in 1936 when urban schools were still the pride of their neighborhoods. These were the places where recent migrants' dreams of the future could become realities. As temples of learning, they were not cheap structures. Expensive materials such as marble, terrazzo, and brass were used freely.

This author visited the school several times beginning in 2004.[17] At that time a fence separated the school from the broken bottles, street trash, and dangers that littered the neighborhood. When approaching the school you wondered if you really wanted to go inside. Then, passing through the gate, something magical happened. Here you walked into a beautiful garden and arboretum that were a cooperative project between the school and a suburban Rotary Club. The main entrance invited you in through large doors with highly shined brass fixtures.

The welcoming atmosphere continued inside the main lobby. Rocking chairs, live plants, fish aquaria, and carts containing books awaited students, parents, and visitors. Walking through the lobby into the main hallway you entered a mysterious world where students work filled the walls and ceilings with artwork to simulate a tropical rainforest. Hallways on all three floors proudly displayed student work. The top floor of the school, in what had been an unused corner, contained a Japanese garden constructed by the school's computer teacher.

Classrooms were filled with learning centers, books, and student work proudly displayed everywhere. Students and teachers were actively engaged in real learning. One classroom in particular stood out. This was a reading recovery room where students experiencing serious reading problems went for special help. The soothing sounds of classical music played in the background. It created a counterpoint to a carpeted room that is alive with books and artwork. A plate of cookies waited on a table for hungry children to help themselves. A very special teacher and her volunteer mother patiently taught children about the mysterious and wonderful world that awaited them in books.

This school was and remains a true oasis, a life-giving center, for a depressed neighborhood. Many failing Philadelphia schools have been taken over by outsider managers, reconstituted by the district because of low achievement, or turned into charter schools. This is not true of Meade. In fact the school exceeds expectations on standardized tests and has been allowed to keep many of its unique arrangements while other schools in the district have been forced to use practices based on centralized models. This school operates on democratic principles that give power for many decisions to teachers most affected by those decisions.

An example of a democratic principle at work was the reduction in class size for the primary grades. Under principal Frank Murphy's guidance, teachers voted on ways to best use funds designated for intervention programs aimed at failing students. Rather than follow the traditional model of hiring student-specific tutors that pulled students from classrooms, they decided to add an additional teacher so as to reduce class sizes for all primary students.

The success of this school can be attributed to dedicated, involved teachers led by the school principal Frank Murphy.[18] Several years ago Murphy began engaging his staff in multiple dialogue sessions aimed at improving the school. Teams designed curricula, set budget priorities, focused on problem students, and worked with parents and the surrounding community to make the school a center for the neighborhood. This same spirit exists in 2021, a true testament to Murphy's influence.[19]

Murphy reached out wherever he could to support these teachers and bring needed resources to the school. Soon after becoming the principal in 1997 he contacted the Philadelphia Writing Project and inquired about becoming involved in a sustained venture to develop literacy skills among his students. This led to the development of a nationally recognized program. Mary Ann Smith, director of governmental relations and public affairs for the National Writing Project, praised Murphy and his staff for "giving students access to the world through literacy."[20]

Another of Murphy's innovations was the development of a partnership with Temple University in Philadelphia. Among the many benefits from this partnership is a project that brings after-school music opportunities to students. Here they are not only exposed to a variety of musical activities but also can learn to play an assortment of instruments.

These examples demonstrate ways that Frank Murphy and his teachers respected the cathedral that they found in each child. David Warner, former editor of *Philadelphia City Paper*, visited Meade as part of a Principal for a Day program. He praised the learning that he found as well as the positive attitude of the principal, teachers, and students. He summarized his visit by writing "If you treat the students with respect, respect is what you get back. If you treat them as test-takers and stuff them into inadequate facilities, a failing school is what you get back."[21]

Meade Elementary is an example of a school where the principal and teachers worked closely with students and parents to achieve success against great obstacles. Theirs was a community effort that manifests the philosophy of John Dewey. They truly did practice his beliefs by placing the well-being of each child in the center of the educational hierarchy. Alienation resulting from learning imposed from outside the child was not an option. At Meade, students did not hate school but welcomed its loving embrace.

Whereas Meade is an example of an entire school manifesting Dewey's child-centered philosophy, the next case illustrates ways a single teacher within a school developed a program aimed at preventing failure, alienation, and hatred among primary-aged students.

A Primary Teacher's Unique Reading Program

It is revealing, perhaps even shocking, to examine the records of high school students who are labeled as potential failures or dropouts. More often than not their problems began in the early primary grades and are usually associated with the acquisition of reading and language arts skills. A primary teacher named Ellen Keys in a rural/suburban district called Midview located outside of Cleveland, Ohio, recognized this fact. She knew that if students experienced failure in the early grades, they not only rejected themselves but became alienated from the system that imposed the failure upon them. She had a better idea and worked hard to provide a learning environment in which all students succeeded.

Fighting against a system that dictated a common reading program for all students, Ellen developed an alternative and convinced her principal to initiate an experimental program in her school. Approximately fifteen kindergarten students who were not ready for phonics-based first-grade reading curriculum were identified. With the consent of their parents, they were placed in a transitional first grade where a unique approach to reading gave them a real chance at success.

Ellen sought aides from several senior citizen volunteers to help her with the program. This was an excellent move as it brought seniors into contact with students whose own grandparents were often absent. It also provided the seniors important contacts with youngsters that were often missing in their lives.

These aides were needed as the reading/language arts program was intensely personal. One particularly interesting activity demonstrates the philosophy used by Ellen. She gave each student a prompt, often regarding animals or pets, and asked them to tell her a brief story about it. Ellen audio-recorded their responses and, working with them over several days, showed them how their spoken words looked when turned into words. The words were placed at the bottom of pages until they resembled a picture book minus the pictures. She then arranged with the high school art teacher to have several of his students illustrate the stories.

Once all the books were illustrated, Ellen organized a luncheon in her classroom that brought together the high school illustrators with the first-grade authors. The menu was simple—vegetable soup prepared by the senior citizens. The atmosphere in the classroom was anything but simple. Both authors and illustrators beamed with warm pride and joy upon meeting each other. Bridging generations by bringing together senior citizens, high school students, and first graders through reading and language arts benefited everyone.

Following the luncheon, each of the books was laminated and put into the school library. Parents and their children were invited in for an evening conference to review student progress. This can be a tense time for teachers, parents, and students. Not this time. As a part of the conference students proudly took their parents into the library and showed them their books.

Rather than hating books and the reading and writing associated with them, these students discovered the joy that can come from investing themselves in a creative project. It is not possible to say that Ellen Keys prevented failures later in these students' school careers. It is also not possible to say that she kept them from feeling alienated from school or the greater society as they grew older. It is possible to say that in this instance she gave them a chance at success and most of them responded favorably.

Ellen may not have known that she was following a philosophy similar to that advocated by John Dewey. She instinctively did know that every child mattered and that each student deserved a personalized education that placed them at the center of the process.[22]

Ellen Keys's classroom represents an example of a single teacher working within a system to make a difference in primary-aged children's lives. The next example illustrates ways that two middle school teachers teamed together to create an unusual program that opened doors for many students who would normally be excluded from such innovative learning opportunities.

Stream Watch: The Way It Should Be

Oftentimes the most engaging and creative programs in our schools are reserved for gifted or academically talented students. Active field experiences, self-directed learning, and engaging experimentation—attributes of many of these programs—are usually reserved for students whose IQ scores or past grades have placed them into special classes taught by the best and most creative teachers.

An unusual middle school program in a rural/suburban Philadelphia school broke the admission barriers for students to enroll in such programs and opened applications for all students. The name of the program was Stream Watch. It proved to be so successful that more than 120 students applied for forty-four spaces, and students were chosen by lottery.

Stream Watch was the brainchild of two middle school teachers, David Jarvie and Tamie Fox, who had a strong interest in placing science education in the center of their sixth- and seventh-grade curriculum. Many of their activities were field-based which led to the name, Stream Watch. Their pedagogy was child-centered and involved active learning that connected with the world outside of the school. As David Jarvie explained it:

> Removing the walls of the classroom was very important to us. Connecting with the outside world and the individuals who were out there making a difference gave the children an opportunity to connect their learning with the real world.[23]

The traditional subjects of reading, writing, and math—usually stressed at the expense of other subjects in today's high-stakes testing environment—were included in their science activities that often integrated geology, biology, chemistry, and meteorology. The program's curriculum revolved around two themes—unity and change. Unity considered the ecological importance of a particular area, and change studied the basic physical elements of watersheds and the environmental impact modern technology has on them. Technical science support was often provided by experts from a regional natural sciences academy.

Through these themes, students explored all subjects. Social studies, for example, received special attention as students studied early Native American history, exploration, wars, and geographic factors that dictate regional economics. As David Jarvie explained: "I still smile today when I think back to the student who would, with a puzzled look on his or her face, say 'I am not sure if this is social studies or science or if this is science or math.'"[24]

The program was highly individualized and stressed independent as well as cooperative learning. Students went into depth on projects and were not constrained from doing so by bells ringing to tell them it was time to switch from one subject to another. They became responsible for their own learning and often graded themselves by developing portfolios using rigorous rubrics created by the teachers. Written narratives of student progress were shared weekly with parents. Students planned their own open-houses and other ways of reporting their progress to parents and the community.

One interesting aspect of the program was that it grouped sixth and seventh graders together into a class of approximately forty-four students. They stayed together for two years and developed a strong sense of community as well as self-discipline. Seventh graders took on leadership roles for the sixth graders. They taught them the science protocols and served as mentors and guides. The power of peer teaching and learning was highly visible.

The Stream Watch program involved extensive community outreach. This led to many unique experiences for students. Some of these included opportunities to meet and hear renowned primatologist Jane Goodall speak about her adventures, climb Neversink Mountain and learn about the history of its trail and railroad, help sail a tall ship on the Delaware River while studying the port of Philadelphia, and meet regularly with prominent environmental scientists.

Students took great pride in the fact that they were part of Stream Watch. One of the reasons for this may have been the positive publicity that the program received from local media. Another may have been the fact that for many of the students it was a unique experience often available only in upper-level groupings.

For most of the students, this experience with independent, student-centered learning freed them to realize greater success than a more traditional text or teacher-centered course. Students who may have been alienated by a conventional educational system were connected and motivated as part of the egalitarian community that they created. The bond between Stream Watch students and their teachers was very strong. Students learned that caring teachers were part of a system that was working for and not against them.

Many students, labeled as potential dropouts, learned a similar lesson in a large suburban high school outside of Cleveland, Ohio. Here, during the early 1970s when both student activism and hostility were often a dominant element in high schools, a dynamic teacher worked to create an innovative communications program aimed specifically at reducing alienation felt by many potential dropouts.

Education through Inquiry

Tom Asad was known as the most creative teacher at Normandy High School in Parma, Ohio.[25] He was an English teacher dedicated to making educational experiences come alive for students who hated school. For example, in teaching William Golding's *Lord of the Flies*, he took students on a weekend field trip into a wilderness area so that they could experience first-hand some of the stresses similar to Golding's schoolboys who were stranded on a deserted island. When teaching poetry he often took students into a candlelit room and gave them quill pens, ink, and fine vellum paper so that they could feel the beauty of words coming from inside them. He simulated some aspects of Big Brother's ever-present surveillance as depicted in George Orwell's *Nineteen Eighty-Four* by having some students spend a night isolated in a TV studio with a camera recording all of their actions.

Tom's activities were often controversial. Normandy was a large high school with, at that time, approximately 2,700 students and 135 teachers. The day that he asked all of his students to demand their IQ scores—scores usually kept secret from students—was one of those times. Counselors were unaware of his demands and when the students began lining up outside their offices they freaked out.

His reputation for both creativity and unusual actions spread into the community. One day a member of the John Birch Society was found in an adjoining classroom secretly recording one of his lessons—presumably hoping to find something damaging enough to get him fired. Even though there were complaints, he was not fired because his actions on behalf of students brought him great respect. Nowhere was this truer than with the Education Through Inquiry or ETI program.

ETI was a program that was team-taught by an English and a social studies teacher at each high school grade to approximately forty students who were labeled as potential dropouts. These were students who were considered of average ability. They were also students who had difficulty in acquiring reading and writing skills that could, in most cases, be traced back to their first years in elementary school. Because they had experienced failure in these basic areas they hated school, were often truant, and when in school were generally discipline problems.

The philosophy behind ETI was simple. No society could afford to lose this type of student. A different way of learning needed to be found for them. ETI teachers, led by Tom Asad, found many alternative methods. These were usually experienced-based and of great interest to students. The teachers referred to this as inductive learning. It involved many field trips, more than twenty per year, as it connected with people in real-life experiences. It also involved deeper connections with targeted members of the community. An example was a unit on drama when students became involved with members of local community theaters and studied all aspects of play production. They then set up their own theater organizations in the classroom that led to productions for themselves as well as other students and teachers in the school.

Another unit of interest dealt with developing expository writing skills through budgeting and meal preparation. ETI students in groups of four or five were given a set budget and had to buy food, prepare a meal in the home economics lab, and serve the food to their classmates. Students had to write out the menus, recipes, and directions in detail. Long before the idea become popular in Iron Chef competitions, they used the technique of having outsiders, often other teachers in the school, judge the quality of their meals.

Tom Asad left Normandy High School and eventually pursued a career as a writer while also teaching in California prisons. Although he has written several books, his most important contributions may well be his years teaching potential dropouts, students who hated school, that they were valued as individuals who did contain a cathedral within. His pedagogy was certainly consistent with the philosophy of John Dewey as he regularly placed students in the center of the power circles and worked hard to make learning important for them. By doing this he eliminated some of the alienation that many felt toward school and society. A testament to the respect and love that students felt toward him was when he was chosen by a graduating class to be their commencement speaker. The applause was thunderous.

Tom Asad is only one example of teachers at Normandy High School who worked hard to bring positive educational experiences to students. Normandy was a place where education was more than a bubble sheet and students were more than statistics. The tone for the school was set by enlightened administrators. Among the best anywhere was the assistant principal, Marty Kane, who was deeply committed to reducing some of the anger and alienation that many students felt toward their school and society in general.[26]

A High School Breakfast Club and Weekend Rides with Police

A dynamic assistant principal named Marty Kane created an unusual high school breakfast club to deal with the anger and alienation experienced by some Normandy High School students. In the early 1970s, many students were riding the wave of the American counter-culture revolution. Normandy was a relatively new high school in Cleveland's largest suburb, Parma. It was a community of middle-class values with strong Eastern European roots and a variety of income levels.

Students represented a range of academic abilities, and, as in many similar schools, there was a group of alienated students who were potential dropouts. They were seen as trouble makers and often had problems with drugs or alcohol. The school's administration consisted of a principal and assistant principal. This seems light by today's standards. Not true in this case. The special personalities and dedication of these two made them real heavyweights by any measure.

Marty worked closely with most student groups in the school. He remarkably learned most of the student's names by studying a number of yearbook pictures in the evening and then finding the students and chatting with them at school the next day. One of his main functions was to deal with potential problems before they became serious crises. One technique that he developed was a breakfast club that included what he called his top thirty students—ten from each class. When a student would leave the group for whatever reason they were replaced by another so that there was always a community of thirty.

He provided breakfast for the top thirty weekly during the school year. At these meetings they talked about school issues, situations ready to erupt, and oftentimes individual difficulties. He tried to see many of these students daily and would talk with them about their progress in school as well as personal problems. If absent from school the student would often receive a phone call at home.

Oftentimes, Marty would learn from breakfast club members about impending problems regarding other students in the school. Several episodes involved planned drinking parties at homes when parents were out of town. These tips led him to develop a close relationship with the city's police, and he would often ride with patrolmen to target destinations to stop potential tragedies. In most cases, crises were avoided, and after stern warnings, the parties either broke up or never occurred at all.

The breakfast club became an inspiration for other programs such as an alternative to traditional school suspensions. Suspension from school is often controversial. It may help the school environment by removing problem students but often does nothing to help the suspended student. Marty developed an alternative program that included day-long sessions for suspended students at a nearby retreat center. For example, all smoking suspensions were held on a certain date at the center. At this time counselors and health experts would work with students individually or in small groups exploring the reasons for smoking and stressing its health dangers. Students suspended for fighting might have sessions on personal anxiety, violence, and related issues.

How many disasters Marty was able to stop through these strategies is impossible to tell. What was observable was the intense loyalty that members of the breakfast club and other alienated students had for him. Theirs was not a community of losers but of winners. He worked hard to combat alienation and the hatred and violence that can grow from it.

Other students in the school held a deep respect for him as well. At a time when most institutional values and the people supporting them were being questioned by the youth, he stood out as a person who cared deeply about students and their education. These feelings extended to the teachers. They knew he valued each of them as much as he valued each student. His actions placed students at the center of the power circles. He inspired teachers to do the same.

The school became known for its innovations. Although it was not articulated that it was based upon John Dewey's progressive philosophy, it clearly was. Actions spoke louder than words, and in this case, practice informs theory. This author was one of the teachers from this school and later became a superintendent in a suburban Philadelphia school district where some of the lessons learned at Normandy High School were put into practice.

Reducing Alienation through a "Motorhead" Club

As seen in the above description, almost every high school has a group of students who feel alienated by the school. For various reasons, they do not quite fit in. They seem to learn best apart from traditional classrooms where desks are in neat rows and questions and answers are in neat boxes. They are often viewed by others as misfits—the ones, who when absent, no one really misses. In many respects, the system gives up and simply warehouses them until they either quit school or graduate near the bottom of the class.

They go by names such as "druggies," "goths," "skaters," or "punks." In a school district near Philadelphia, they were known as "Motorheads." Soon after arriving, the new superintendent in the Owen J. Roberts School District decided to reach out to them in hopes that their alienation would not turn into hatred and violence.

The superintendent's office overlooked the high school parking lot. From this vantage point, it was possible to see a lineup of beautifully reconditioned cars that were parked in a section reserved, through unwritten rules, for the Motorheads. These students were usually the first ones to leave school and generally raced out of the parking lot while lighting up a much-craved cigarette.

A speed bump near the entrance to the superintendent's office slowed the traffic, and one day the superintendent went out and stopped the first car, a shiny yellow 1971 Plymouth, as it slowed over the bump. He identified myself to the driver, a young man of about seventeen who quickly shoved a cigarette up his sleeve. After explaining an interest in his car, the superintendent asked if the young man would show him the engine the next day at about the same time. Startled and relieved the driver said he would.

The next day the student proudly raised the hood to show a modified engine that was better than showroom-clean. A group of approximately twenty other Motorheads (mostly male but many accompanied by their female friends) were there as well. They began a conversation about cars—and about school. These students said that they had a tough time sitting in classes. They considered them unimportant. They found most lectures to be dull. They often slept in class.

A famous John Dewey quotation came to the superintendent's mind: "What the best and wisest parent wants for his own child, that must the community want for all of its children."[27] Field trips, exciting speakers, and experience-based learning were not usually available for these students. The system dictated the what, when, and how of their learning.

That afternoon things began to change. Asked if they would be interested in coming together periodically to learn through field trips and other hands-on experiences, the students responded enthusiastically. This was the beginning of the Motorhead Club that included approximately thirty members and lasted for several years.

Over the years, the club did many interesting things together. One of the first, as might be expected, was to attend a car race together. Members also experienced academics in different ways. One of these involved learning about Iraq and the birth of civilization by visiting a distinguished linguist at the University of Pennsylvania's Museum of Archaeology and Anthropology.

This rare scholar was compiling a dictionary of ancient Sumerian words from the vast collection of cuneiform tablets in the museum's archives. These tablets were not normally open to the public. After becoming familiar with the collection, the superintendent called the director and arranged a visit for a group of high school students. They were not identified as Motorheads.

In preparation for the field trip the students met for several sessions during which they learned about the geography of Iraq, viewed portions of *Legacy: The Origins of Civilization* regarding ancient Mesopotamia, and tasted Middle Eastern food. Arrangements were made for a school bus to take them into the city and for lunch following the museum visit. There were no costs to the students—they were paid for from a special superintendent salary giveback fund. No special instructions were given regarding dress for the trip, and it was a pleasant surprise when the students arrived with men wearing ties and women in dresses.

When the Motorheads arrived at the museum, Dr. Erle Leichty, director of the Sumerian dictionary project, took them into a workroom containing a large number of cabinets and files. It was here that students learned about the land of Eden in present-day Iraq and the epic of Gilgamesh. The 5,000-year-old Gilgamesh legend is of a hero-wanderer who sought eternal life. He found the plant that would give it to him at the bottom of the sea—only to have it stolen by a serpent. Gilgamesh learned the lesson that eternal life is not found on this earth.

Members of the Motorhead Club were able to hold some of the ancient tablets in their hands. As students were passing tablets from hand to hand, Dr. Leichty said that one of the largest (approximately dinner-plate size), then being held by the leader of the club, was the centerpiece of the collection. The student asked what it was and learned that this was the earliest written record of the flood story—Noah's ark.

This was an awestruck Hollywood moment reminiscent of *Raiders of the Lost Ark*. Imagine, a forgotten Motorhead from an average school district holding a historical artifact of immeasurable value in his greased-stained hands. Lightning bolts, indeed. On this day, these students learned about history by experiencing something very deep and profoundly real. Few would soon forget this encounter with the past.

The club experienced many other learning activities that had an impact on them. One involved a visit to the New Jersey shore to go on a whale-watching adventure. This activity was motivated by a student who hated school and loved to spend time at the shore. He planned the trip, and in preparation for it, the Motorheads read and discussed Ernest Hemingway's *The Old Man and the Sea*. Though they did not see any whales on their voyage they did see many other types of fish and experienced a few hours of life on the sea.

Years later, this author received a letter from the young man who planned the trip. After barely graduating from high school, he went to Florida to pursue life on the beach. He later enrolled in a community college and eventually turned those two years into a four-year degree. His degree was in elementary education.

Other Motorheads wrote letters as well. Some told of going into various branches of the military or shared news of becoming parents. It is possible, maybe even probable, that many of the Motorheads may have survived school and become productive citizens without the intervention of the club. It is also possible that an elementary teacher in Florida and a sailor on board an American ship at sea may not have. America would have been the poorer for the loss. The time, effort, and money were worth the gamble.

SUMMARY: LESSONS LEARNED

- A philosophy that views students as black slates and an almost absolute focus on high-stakes testing can lead to student alienation and the potential for violence.
- A contrasting child-centered philosophy that recognizes the inherent beauty and importance of each student can lead to rich educational experiences that reduce student alienation and the potential for violence.
- Teachers and other educational leaders with a strong sense of agency as well as creativity provide examples of experiences that nourish all students.

The educators presented in this chapter can be considered as transformational educational leaders. The next chapter, "Transformational Leadership," defines the meaning of this often elusive term by considering the central concepts of transformational leadership to be mission, vision, and community. To successfully create transformational change, the three elements—though distinctive—need to be viewed as one entity so that the whole becomes greater than the sum of its parts.

NOTES

1. Mark Obmascik, "Massacre at columbine high, Bloodbath leaves 15 dead, 28 hurt," *Denver Post*, April 21, 1999, http://extras.denverpost.com/news/shot0420a.htm (accessed January 4, 2018).

2. Lori Rozsa, Moriah Balingit, William Wan and Mark Berman, "'A horrific, horrific day': At least 17 killed in Florida school shooting," *The Washington Post*, February 15, 2018 (accessed February 23, 2018).

3. Ralph Ellis, Eric Levenson and Andrea Diaz, "Aztec high school shooting: 2 slain students identified," *CNN*, December 8, 2017, http://www.cnn.com/2017/12/07/us/aztec-high-school-shooting-new-mexico/index.html (accessed January 4, 2018).

4. "Education week's 2020 school shooting tracker," *Education Week*, September 2, 2021, https://www.edweek.org/leadership/school-shootings-this-year-how-many-and-where/2021/03 (accessed September 5, 2021).

5. Comments shared with the author by an elementary school principal during a 2015 educational leadership class at Saint Joseph's University.

6. Charlie Chaplin (writer, director), *Modern Times* (United States: United Artists, 1936), Movie.

7. The author knows of several situations in the Philadelphia School District as well as suburban districts where teachers have been transferred and principals have lost their jobs because of a failure to meet annual testing goals.

8. Freeden Oeurr, email message to author, December 20, 2004.

9. Joseph Clark, former Owen J. Roberts elementary school principal, conversation with author, February 21, 2008.

10. John Locke, *An Essay Concerning Human Understanding* (London: 1690), http://www.earlymoderntexts.com/assets/pdfs/locke1690book1.pdf (accessed January 4, 2018).

11. Jean Jacques Rousseau, Roger Maters, ed., Judith Masters, tr., *On the Social Contract* (New York: St. Martin's Press, 1978), 46.

12. Jean Jacques Rousseau and Allan Bloom, tr., *Emile or on Education* (New York: Basic Books, 1979), 37.

13. The anecdote of Schweitzer was one that was presented at an A.S.C.D. conference keynote speech delivered by Norman Cousins on March 21, 1977. This author attended and took notes on his presentation.

14. John Dewey recognized the dialectic between these two forces in his 1938 book *Experience and Education* (New York: Macmillan Publishing, 1938, 1963). He wrote "The history of educational theory is marked by opposition between the idea that education is development from within and that it is formation from without (p. 17)." In 1916 he labeled this dialectic as nurture versus nature when he stated in *Democracy and Education* (New York: Macmillan Publishing, 1916, 1966) that "great as is the significance of nurture, of modification, and transformation through direct educational effort, nature, or unlearned capacities, affords the foundation and ultimate resources for such nurture" (p. 117).

15. John Dewey, *The School and the Society, The Child and the Curriculum* (Chicago: The University of Chicago Press, 1900, 1990), 187.

16. In *Democracy and Education* (New York: Macmillan Company: 1916, 1966), John Dewey wrote: "Such a [democratic] society must have a type of education which gives individuals a personal interest in social relationships and control, and habits of mind which secure social changes without introducing disorder" (p. 99).

17. This author made several visits to Meade elementary school in research for *Combating Hatred: Educators Leading the Way* (Lanham, MD: Rowman & Littlefield, 2009). This account is based primarily on those visits. However, recent research indicates that this account is also substantially accurate in 2021.

18. Frank Murphy retired in 2010. Many of the innovations that he brought to this school remain as of this writing (2021). See http://thenotebook.org/latest0/2010/06/30/f-goes-public (accessed January 21, 2018), regarding his retirement, and http://webgui.phila.k12.pa.us/schools/m/meade (accessed January 21, 2018).

19. The 2021 website for Mede Elementary is https://meade.philasd.org/.

20. Mary Ann Smith, "National writing project, it takes a school," *The Voice*, vol. 9, no. 3 http://www.nwp.org/cs/public/print/resource/1960?x-print_friendly=1 (accessed January 4, 2018).

21. David Warner, "Someplace special," *Citypaper.net*, December 19-25, 2002, http://www.citypaper.net/articles/2002-12-19/slant2.shtml (accessed January 18, 2008).

22. The account of Ellen Keyes is a direct first-hand account, while this author was superintendent of the Midview school district (1979–1986).

23. David Jarvie, e-mail message to author, February 8, 2008.

24. Ibid.

25. This author worked for six years with Tom Asad at Normandy High School. These accounts have been verified by Asad.

26. This author worked with Mary Kane for six years at Normandy High School. These accounts have been verified by Kane.

27. John Dewey, *The School and the Society, The Child and the Curriculum* (Chicago: The University of Chicago Press, 1990), 7.

Chapter 6

Transformational Leadership

The transactional leader function[s] as a broker.[1]

But to transform something . . . is to cause a metamorphosis in form or structure, a change in the very condition or nature of a thing . . . radical change in outward form or inner character.[2]

—James MacGregor Burns

DEFINING TRANSFORMATIONAL LEADERSHIP

Transformational leadership is an elusive concept. Even though it is difficult to provide a precise definition, we usually know when we are engaged with transformational leaders. These are the times when our intellects are buzzing with fresh ideas fueled with new perspectives; times when our emotions are bursting and carry us to places we have not been before. These are the times when individual identities are lost in a true democratic community, times in which the roles of leaders and followers often become indistinct as they grow together toward a common vision nurtured by a common mission.

Those seeking to become transformational educational leaders often assume some magic formula can be the catalyst that transforms them, one that can be easily replicated. There is no such formula. To understand the concept of transformational leadership better, individuals can examine several studies beginning with James MacGregor Burns's 1978 Pulitzer Prize–winning book *Leadership* in which he promotes the terms "transforming" or "transformational leadership." In this book and its 2003 companion, *Transforming Leadership*, he analyzed several major historical world figures and drew from them qualities, situations, and actions that he felt distinguished them as transformational leaders.

Burns's clearest definition of transformational leadership occurs when he contrasts it with transactional leadership. He defines transactional leadership as political give-and-take in which leaders negotiate from different power positions and trade favors to accomplish objectives.[3]

By contrast, transformational leadership can be far more significant and cause fundamental changes that involve a metamorphosis in form or structure.[4] Burns described transformational leaders as those who are able to inspire others to help accomplish such changes. He ends *Transforming Leadership* this way:

> In the broadest terms, transforming change flows not from the work of the "great man" who single-handedly makes history, but from the collective achievement of "great people." While leadership is necessary at every stage beginning with the first spark that awakens people's hopes, its vital role is to create and expand the opportunities that empower people to pursue happiness for themselves.[5]

Several scholars, such as Bernard Bass and Kenneth Leithwood, have added to Burns's groundbreaking work and advanced our understanding of the concept.[6] Rather than examine the works of Burns, Bass, Leithwood, and others in greater detail, let us follow a different approach, one similar to that employed by Burns, and examine eight case studies of educators in a variety of positions and settings who can be defined as transformational educational leaders. Before presenting their case studies, let us look more deeply at three key elements essential for transformational changes to occur.

KEY ELEMENTS OF TRANSFORMATIONAL LEADERSHIP—MISSION, VISION, AND COMMUNITY

Educational leaders who are successful in combating hatred are those who embrace the central concepts of transformational leadership—mission, vision, and community. To successfully create transformational change, the three elements—though distinctive—need to be viewed as one entity so that the whole becomes greater than the sum of its parts. Imagine that the image seen here is alive with dynamic energy flowing between the three segments of the circle (figure 6.1).

Examining each of the key elements separately can give us an in-depth realization of the dynamic whole. It is similar to viewing the graphic in 3-D. Let us begin by probing deeply into the most important of the three—mission. We will begin by examining the opening scenes of the 1986 movie *Mission*.

Transformational Leadership

Figure 6.1 Essential Qualities of Mission, Vision, and Community. *Source*: Author Created.

Mission

Mission—the movie starring Jeremy Irons, Robert De Niro, and Liam Neeson—deservedly won, among other top international awards, the Cannes Film Festival Palme d'Or in 1986.[7] It is a deeply intense depiction of the Jesuits' mid-eighteenth-century missionary activity. It was then that they engaged with the native Guaraní in the tropical rainforests that today comprise parts of Argentina, Brazil, and Paraguay. The dramatic opening of the movie shows Fr. Julian, bound crucifixion style to a cross, being thrown by some Guaraní into a swiftly flowing river. The rapids surge to the precipice of the Iguazu Falls and hurl Fr. Julian to his death 269 feet below.

Fr. Gabriel (Jeremy Irons) and two companion Jesuits recover the body and determine once again to encounter the Guaraní above the Falls. Fr. Gabriel says that he will make the climb as it was he who sent Fr. Julian on this mission.

With his oboe in a cloth pack on his back, Gabriel begins the climb. It is torturously slow—step by step by step, bare feet on chiseled rocks, water crashing all around. Slipping and nearly falling to his death, he finally reaches the solid ground above the Iguazu. Venturing into the dark green/black rainforest dripping with humidity, he recoils as he spots an iguana hanging from a tree. A few more steps. A branch cracks. Gabriel and some Guaraní come face to face. No formalities here—just muted shock and fear all around. Then Gabriel unpacks his oboe.

With soothing music, he fascinates some of the Guaraní while others are determined that he should have a fate similar to Fr. Julian. Eventually, he is accepted among them, and thus begins the Jesuit missions into this area of South America. Here they established "reducciones"—safe fort-like havens for Guaraní as required by Spanish law. The hope was to protect them from Portuguese slave catchers and mercenaries. The Jesuits, however, were no match for the Portuguese who team up with some Spanish forces and eventually capture or kill most of the reduccciones' inhabitants.

Though only a movie, the depiction is based upon actual events. These raise two serious questions for us today.

- What is the fire that burned deep within each of these Jesuits?
- What is it that caused them to abandon the temporal life and risk everything for their spiritual beliefs?

It was then, and is today, a strong sense of mission: the belief that theirs was and is a special relationship with Jesus Christ gained through the Spiritual Exercises of Saint Ignatius. That bond outshone and today continues to outshine every otherworldly passion. In poker terms, they were and are "all in."

Using this example of what "mission" can mean, transformational educators need to assess their personal sense of mission. If you hope to be such a leader, go deeply into your inner self and ask these questions:

- What is it that drives and motivates me as I aspire to be a true transformational leader?
- What is it that ignites a fire in the innermost part of my being?

Educational leaders who are successful in combating hatred are those who not only experience but also embrace the central and most important concept of transformational leadership—mission. A strong sense of mission—both personal and collective—will, however, remain barren unless it becomes translated into a specific vision.

Vision

Successful transformational change requires that vision statements and actions flow from and build upon both the personal and collective mission of the organization. The vision is usually more specific than the mission and should be tightly aligned with it. Educational examples that grow from student-centered mission statements could be:

- a curriculum that places students at the center of experiential learning;
- an all-inclusive curriculum that bridges racial divides;
- free summer-camp experiences for students who are economically distressed;
- field experiences that are made vital for all teachers and students;

- experiences that expand the school's boundaries to include the greater community's rich cultural resources;
- educational spaces that physically shape and bring to life the basic elements of the school and district's mission.

Let us explore more deeply the idea of a vision fulfilling the mission through the design and construction of a new school. The Owen J. Roberts school district needed a new elementary school to replace its North Coventry building which had been built in 1912. The age of the building plus an increased population presented an opportunity to design a school that reflected in brick and mortar the district's student-centered mission statement.

District leaders searched for an architectural firm that was willing to provide something radically different from the normal process of designing a school. First, the architects needed to be both artists and engineers. They had to believe in bringing to life the ancient Roman architect Vitruvius's three essential elements for high-road architecture—fitness, firmness, and delight. To do this, they had to agree to provide a yearlong course for all of the school's teachers and leaders in architectural theory, design, and basic construction. They had to agree to transparency and interact regularly with parents, students, and various community members.

A highly respected firm was found that met the district's criteria. A nine-month course was developed for teachers and district leaders that included both philosophical and practical experiences. Nearly 100 percent of the teachers attended the course for which they were paid a stipend or received university credit.

The course included rigorous readings and practical sessions where teachers worked alongside architectural designers.[8] Visitations were made to avant-garde schools in Pennsylvania and neighboring states. Rich dialogue sessions grew from these readings and visitations—sessions that breathed life into the district and school's student-centered mission statement.

The final design included spaces for small- and large-group interaction, creative arts, and media/technology centers. The school was enveloped by overall pleasing aesthetics that reflected the surroundings of the rural/suburban neighborhood. In many instances, new curricula were developed, and many teachers adopted diverse pedagogies as their interaction with the new spaces gave different perspectives to the school's mission. Most importantly, the course turned a miscellaneous group of elementary educators into a vibrant community of learners whose focus was the well-being of all students.

This strong sense of community extended to the parents and students who were excited about the opening of their new school. One example demonstrates this sense of community. The school was set to open the day after Labor Day. The week prior was to be move-in time for teachers.

Unfortunately, there was a delay in getting all of the building permits. They were not received until the Friday before Labor Day.

Almost miraculously the building principal worked with teachers and the local parent-teacher association to organize the final cleaning and move-in of the school. Special note—this occurred over the Labor Day weekend when many vacation plans had to be altered. Parents and teachers all wanted the first day for students to be special and on time. It happened. Welcoming smiles greeted excited students and everyone involved was filled with pride. The mission was fulfilled in a very special way through the realization of the vision of a new school.

The sense of community was inspiring to everyone. As a measure of gratitude to the community and teachers, school leaders decided to hold a special dedication for the new school. They organized it to be held the week prior to Thanksgiving. The superintendent donated money to provide a turkey dinner for everyone in the community. The parent-teachers association organized potluck dishes to augment the feast. Nearly 500 students, parents, teachers, and community members attended the celebration.

The entire North Coventry experience—from design to dedication—demonstrates ways that a vision grew from a mission. This example raises important questions for those hoping to be transformational leaders:

- What particular inspirations do I have that can lead to visions which manifest my sense of mission?
- How can I lead in developing specific strategic plans that will achieve specific visions?

It also demonstrates the power of community which we will now examine in more detail.

The Power of Community

Imagine that you are either a member of the Permian High School football team or a fan in the new 19,000 seat stadium. You are experiencing a "Mojo" football game as described by H.G. "Buzz" Bissinger in *Friday Night Lights*. His 1990 book, later made into a movie and television series, captures the excitement of Texas football as the Permian Panthers from Odessa, Texas fight for the state championship.

Bissinger was intrigued when he discovered that a new multimillion dollar stadium was built to house more than 19,000 fans in a town of only 100,000 people. A prize-winning journalist with the *Philadelphia Inquirer*, he decided he needed a piece of the action and took his wife and two boys to live in Odessa for nearly one year.

During that time he interviewed players, parents, teachers, students, and community members so as to capture the essence of what small-town football meant in not just Odessa but America as well. His book was controversial—after publication he reported to having received several death threats. Bissinger portrayed the passion for football in Odessa as close to a religion. He described educators favoring the team's players with easy multiple-choice tests and low-level academic expectations.

Friday Night Lights is filled with passion which is dramatically captured by Bissinger as he brings to life the sense of community created not only on the field but in the stands as fans focused every second of every minute of every hour on one thing—winning a football game. Perhaps you can hear the roar of the crowd as black-and-white clad cheerleaders invoke various calls and yells. Perhaps you can smell and feel the heat of the crowd as a fever pitch is reached after a touchdown wins a close game. This is what community is about: unity + common purpose = community.

Imagine another example. You are a volunteer member of the world-famous Mormon Tabernacle Choir. Your audition was stress-filled as you competed with hundreds of others to be in this magnificent ensemble. Now you work full time, juggle family responsibilities, and travel nearly 100 miles to Thursday night rehearsals and then again to Sunday worship services. Then there are the performances outside of Salt Lake City. The Choir is in high demand and performances have included world fairs, Olympic Games, White House concerts, international festivals, and hundreds of other prestigious events.

The wear and tear on your life melts away, however, when the conductor, Mack Wilberg, raises his hand and, as one voice, all 360 of you sign the "Battle Hymn of the Republic," " How Great Thou Art," "Amazing Grace," or some other stirring composition. For certain, there are goosebumps on your arms and legs—community, indeed. Here we experience unity + common purpose = community. Community is the fuel that propels both the mission and the vision.

The difference between these two community experiences is the common mission and vision of each example. In the first example, we have "Mojo" football: mission—high school football; vision—state championship. This is compared to the Mormon Tabernacle Choir: mission—singing deeply inspired music as an expression of God's love in the world; vision—worship services and specific worldwide performances.

These two examples pose important questions for educators hoping to be transformational leaders:

- How can I lead in creating a strong community whose core values are based upon a common mission?

- How can I lead a community to define and achieve common visions that manifest our mission?

For educators, especially those who hope to be transformational, the lessons to be learned from the unity of the mission-vision-community dynamic are enormous.

SUMMARY—LESSONS LEARNED

This chapter presents a definition of transformational leadership as differentiated from transactional leadership—a distinction provided by James MacGregor Burns in his book *Transforming Leadership*. It develops three key components of transformational leadership as follows:

- mission,
- vision, and
- community.

Each of these components is developed in-depth with practical examples provided so that theory and practice are combined. The union of the three—mission, vision, and community—are a powerful force that enable leaders to become transformational.

Let us learn more about this unity as we look in chapter 7, "Inspirational Transformational Educational Leaders," at some specific examples of educators whose experiences capture the essence of transformational leadership. These examples are not nationally well-known "stars" but rather educators whose day-to-day activities on the frontlines of educational change contain important lessons for educators everywhere. This author has been inspired by all of them and has worked alongside many of them as they became transformational and combated hatred in their own unique ways.

NOTES

1. James MacGregor Burns, *Transforming Leadership* (New York: Atlantic Monthly Press, 2003), 24.
2. Ibid.
3. James MacGregor Burns elaborates on this definition of transactional leadership on page 24 in his *Transforming Leadership* when he wrote that it is the "daily stuff of politics, the pursuit of change in measured and often reluctant doses." He describes such a leader further in the same work and on the same page as follows:

"The transactional leader functioned as a broker and, especially when the stakes were low, his role could be relatively minor, even automatic."

4. James MacGregor Burns distinguishes between the verbs "change" and "transform" attributing "change" to transactional leadership and "transform" to transformational leadership. He wrote on page 24 of *Transforming Leadership*: "To change is to substitute one thing for another, to give and take, to exchange places, to pass from one place to another. These are the kinds of changes I attribute to transactional leadership. But to transform something cuts much more profoundly. It is to cause a metamorphosis in form or structure, a change in the very condition or nature of a thing, a change into another substance, a radical change in outward form or inner character, as when a frog is transformed into a prince or a carriage maker into an auto factory. It is change of this breadth and depth that is fostered by transforming leadership."

5. Burns, *Transforming Leadership*, 240.

6. Burns has elevated the study of democratic leadership from the publication of books and articles to sustained research through organizations such as the James MacGregor Burns Academy of Leadership based at the University of Maryland. His influence is extensive and has inspired many leadership theorists who have expanded on his work. Two of the key writers among these theorists are Bernard Bass and Kenneth Leithwood. Examples of their publications are as follows: Bass, *Leadership and Performance Beyond Expectations*, 1985; *Improving Organizational Effectiveness Through Transformational leadership*, with Bruce J. Avolio, 1994); Leithwood, "The Move Toward Transformational Leadership," *Educational Leadership*, 1992; *Changing Leadership for Changing Times*, with Doris Jantzi and Rosanne Steinbach, 1999).

7. An excellent guide to the movie is found on the University of Scranton website at: https://www.scranton.edu/the-jesuit-center/mission-film-guide.shtml.

8. Philosophical aspects of the course included readings by Michel Foucault, Robert Venturi, Robert A.M. Stern, Witold Rybczynski, and Lois Kahn. Practical experiences included field experiences to the architects' Harrisburg offices where teachers worked alongside professional designers developing ideas that would bring to life the district's student-centered mission. Visitations were also made to see avante-garde schools in Pennsylvania and other states.

Chapter 7

Inspirational Transformational Educational Leaders

"The greatest teachers:
   Light paths that grow from veiled darkness;
   Touch secrets deep within breathing souls;
   Explode minds into universes unknown;
   Transform themselves and unbelieving worlds."[1]

—Terrance Furin

Transformational educational leaders are those who in deeply profound ways create meaningful change by leading lives that inspire others to be better than they thought they were. Their very presence exudes passions that grow from core social justice values. As leaders, they create vibrant communities bound together by a common mission as they strive to achieve common visions. The following eight examples are such transformational educational leaders. They cover a broad range of experiences, ages, races, and genders. What they have in common is their ability to combat hatred and change worlds.

Because the art of teaching is at the core of all transformational leadership, we will begin by looking at an extraordinary classroom teacher. His name is Michael (Mike) Wall. He is an extraordinary teacher and an author.

MICHAEL WALL: TEACHER AND AUTHOR

Mike Wall's thirty-six years in the classroom were not enough for him. Since his formal retirement in 2011, he has continued to write inspirational thoughts, essays, and poetry on his website entitled Every Good Morning. He is, truly, a transformational educational leader.

Chaos at a School Board Meeting

The first time that this author met Mike Wall was at an August 1990 school board meeting in the Owen J. Roberts school district located forty-five miles from Philadelphia. The meeting was held in a 500-seat auditorium that was filled with hatred: standing room only; reporters from major Philadelphia TV stations sending messages to vans in the parking lot that would transmit them to hungry viewers; photographers crouching, then standing to get multi-angled shots; baskets being passed through the crowd to collect money for a legal battle—all of this and much more because the Jewish valedictorian at the recent commencement did not want Christian prayer at her graduation.

A new district superintendent had come the previous month from Ohio. This author was that new kid in town who received a warning from the outgoing superintendent—"do not touch the school prayer issue, it will consume you."[2] His knowledge of school law and various Supreme Court decisions told him otherwise. Working with the district's leadership team and gathering input from both national and state school board associations, new policies were created that banned prayer in classrooms and at all school-sponsored events. A final school board vote on those policies is what led to the contentious meeting in August.

Public comment regarding the policies raged for more than two-and-a-half hours. Threats and warnings of dire consequences were hatefully made. School board members, the board solicitor, and the school superintendent were seated at a long table on the floor of the auditorium in close proximity to the heated crowd. One of the eight board members passed a note to the superintendent—"could the vote be delayed?" A one-word note was returned with the answer—"no." The board voted 8–0 to adopt the new policies. Mayhem erupted.

It was evident that nearly everyone in the crowd was opposed to the new policies. Near the end of the public comment session, one person stood and spoke in their favor. His name was Mike Wall. The name meant nothing to the new superintendent. What did have meaning was that here was someone who had an enormous amount of courage—in the heat of that public forum, no less. He did not know that Mike was held in the highest regard by his colleagues, students, and community members who knew him. As an English teacher and chair of the department, he had earned a reputation for being courageous in tough situations. Let us learn more.

An Encounter with Tall Boy and Long Hair

Courage alone is not enough. For Mike, courage was not an end but a means to an end. This was demonstrated early in his teaching career. He relates on his website that during his fourth day as a new high school teacher he had to break up a vicious fight between two high school students that he names "Long Hair" and "Tall Boy." Actually, it was not a fight but a pounding of Long Hair by Tall Boy. Mike saw this, and his adrenaline kicked in. He forced his way through the crowd of students who were watching the beating and forcefully separated the two young men. His anger landed especially hard on Tall Boy.[3]

Grabbing both boys, Mike led Long Hair to the nurse while he and Tall Boy went to the principal's office. When the principal asked whether Mike had hurt him or had sworn at him, Tall Boy responded: "He didn't say nothin'."[4] An unspoken bond was forged.

Mike did not realize at the time that Tall Boy was the "Alpha" of a high school group known as the "Motorheads." This was a group of high-schoolers, who when absent, caused teachers relief, if not outward cheering. Beyond socialization, they viewed school as having little value for them. They could not get out of there fast enough. At the end of the day, they were the ones racing to their reconditioned cars to light up the first of many cigarettes.

Confronting Tall Boy earned Mike the respect of not only Tall Boy and the Motorheads but of his colleagues as well. After the incident, many of them were anxious to hear the details at the local pub. And, oh, yes—later Mike became the faculty advisor of the Motorhead Club. He opened himself and his classroom to them and their many, many needs.

Profound Love of Teaching

Beneath Mike's strong courage lies a profound layer of empathy based on real social justice values that not only find but celebrate the cathedral within each person. He has deep protective love for his students, past and present. He has an even greater love for what it means to be a true teacher. He shares this on his website as he reflects on his beginnings as a teacher:

> Romeo was right. Just like that I fell in love. No other word is adequate to explain what I felt in the classroom whether I was lecturing, doing question and answer or working with kids individually. All of it was . . . pure, as if a new dimension to my life had been added in one crackling moment of contact. Nothing had ever made me happier.[5]

He continues to describe his feelings on becoming a teacher this way:

Most importantly, I recognized that I liked people. That sounds strange. It's not. How many teachers have you known who do not like human beings? Now think about that number you just calculated.

I liked teenage people especially—their idealism, goofiness, ability to set fires in an instant, their uncertainties and quests, their willingness to take chances, the exquisite seismograph of their sensitivities, their limitless capacity for laughter, their powerful bullshit detectors, their innocence even at their most cynical.[6]

Transformational Educational Leader

There is no doubt about his courage, empathy, and love of teaching his students. Mike was a leader—a transformational leader—not only in the classroom but beyond it as well. One episode in particular is worth noting.

Mike had developed a special bond with one of his high school principals, Bill Faulkner. It was Bill who informed the new superintendent that it was Mike Wall who spoke on behalf of the revised school prayer policy. Three years later, in 1993, Bill and Mike meet with the superintendent and asked about the possibility of developing an interdisciplinary course on the Holocaust.

The superintendent readily agreed and arranged for some meetings to plan the course. A crucial first step would be to develop a series of professional development sessions for high school teachers. Mike, Bill, and the superintendent took a trip that summer to the Holocaust museum in Washington, D.C., to gather ideas and generate possibilities for a professional development course that would last an entire school year.

The course with monthly sessions was attended by nearly 100 percent of the high school teachers.[7] A highlight was the faculty field trip to the Holocaust museum in Washington—lots of chatter among colleagues on the way down; near silence on the way home. What is significant here regarding Mike is the leadership that he showed in proposing the idea, developing the course, and following through with his colleagues on its implementation.

The course paid special dividends as high school teachers felt empowered to combat hatred when a neo-Nazi group proposed a boycott of schools (see chapter 4, "Combating a Neo-Nazi Hate Group"). They developed curricula for the day of the boycott and assisted teachers at the middle and elementary levels to do the same. When the day arrived, Mike and other teachers were in the parking lot greeting students as they arrived at school. His presence along with his colleagues assured the students that their day at school would be a safe one filled with rich learning about neo-Nazis and their presence in America. A teachable moment, indeed.

Mike the Author and Poet

Mike's passion for teaching and rich engagement with others did not end with his retirement from the classroom. In June 2011, he began writing on his website *Every Good Morning*. As of September 2021, he had made 716 postings covering various topics. He lists these on the site as "Books and ideas, Family, Home, Nature, People, Teaching High school Students and Travel."

The listing does not begin to capture the uniqueness of the various topics. For example, post 715 deals with his experiences in getting a haircut. Other posts deal with the most pressing national and international topics. Mike's writings after the Sandy Hook school massacre or the January 6 Capitol riot engage you at the core and come from an inner strength that hits you in the gut.

Among the most insightful and lyrical of the postings are his descriptions of writing poetry. Here is one from post # 716:

> Poetry feels like writing forced through multiple filters. That is true of all writing. Filters are meant to remove impurities, extraneous mush, that which does not belong. But prose operates with both addition and subtraction, with both purification and embellishment, while poetry feels like each filter is of a smaller gauge than the one above it, so that as the revision process goes on, what emerges is cleaner, clearer, more exact, more defined, the images sharper, the verbs and nouns more solid in the weight of associations they are meant to carry. It feels like writing driven ruthlessly toward both brevity and density simultaneously, as if one is compressing a star. You want the most brilliant light to emerge from the most precise form.[8]

Mike's own poetry is similar to the compression of a star where "you want the most brilliant light to emerge from the most precise form." An example is found in his poem entitled "Inishmore." As background, Inishmore is one of Ireland's Aran Islands in Galway Bay. Mike and his wife Patti visited it early on a misty morning. Here are his words:

Golden light aglow like halos
in bad pictures never works for revelations.
For those look up to high, white light,
the translucent early morning,
a white obsidian eastern brand.

In a chapel I could cross in four steps
fishermen in wool coats stood enormously

singing hymns in Gaelic, their mothers and wives
black-shawled miniatures by their sides.

The priest before us had closed his eyes,
his tenor voice rising above the rest,
a bright ribbon turning round the air.

The singing language I could not understand
gentled in me, one more light from far-flung stars
forever passing through.

We stood together in the sound of waves,
this meeting of bodies and song,
and the light poured into us
steady as a stream in full flush of rain.[9]

His love of language and the power that words can have in sharing experiences and creating emotions is evident in his writing.

On his first day of student teaching nearly fifty years ago, he nervously introduced *The Great Gatsby* to a group of high school students. The passion he had for teaching then is still evident today. It is probable that Mike could have had any number of administrative jobs over the years. Instead, he chose to remain a classroom teacher. His chosen path is an inspiration.

Mike's qualities as a true transformational educator and leader can be summarized as follows:

- Mission—his strong passion for teaching both inside and outside of the classroom reveals his deep love of humanity;
- Vision—his strong sense of mission has been and continues to be manifested in several visions built upon his unique abilities to engage high school students and members of the greater public;
- Community—he has created innumerable communities of learners through his sensitive writing and continuous yearning to discover new experiences and ideas to share with others.

The next transformational leader who exemplifies the qualities of mission, vision, and community is a young elementary teacher named Tiara Grymes. Tiara was frustrated with the lack of multicultural literary experiences for students of color in multicultural classrooms. She did something about this. She got a doctorate from Saint Joseph's University. Her dissertation centered on ways to use professional development to increase White elementary teachers' sense of self-efficacy in using multicultural literature inside of the classroom.

TIARA GRYMES: TEACHER AND TEACHER COACH

Tiara began teaching in a Philadelphia Catholic school in the fall of 2015. After one year in that position, she became a grade 4/5 classroom teacher in the Philadelphia School District. In August 2019, Tiara began a new position as a teacher coach and fourth-grade teacher at a Philadelphia charter school named Green Woods Charter.

Green Woods Elementary Charter School

Charter schools are a special category of public schools. While still receiving funds from the public school district, they are relieved of many of the regulations that govern the public schools. Charter schools are popular in Philadelphia. For the 2021–2022 school year, the total school enrollment for Philadelphia was 202,944 students. Of this number, 68,364 were in charter schools. Charters are schools with particular missions that focus on certain aspects of student learning that may not be as dominant in the general public schools.[10]

For example, a school may have a mission to be highly Afro-centric where language arts classes, in addition to teaching English, include various African languages and emphasize African art forms. Another example might be a charter that uses a tightly scripted curriculum which emphasizes standardized tests tied to the Common Core national standards. Tiara's school, Green Woods Charter, is student-centered with an emphasis on experiential learning. Green Woods Charter has a population of 674 with 68.4 percent being White, 18.7 percent Black, 3.9 percent Hispanic, 1.3 percent Asian, 0.6 percent American Indian or Alaskan, and 7 percent two or more races.[11]

Such a multicultural school can be a blessing if it celebrates the cultural diversity of its students. Such a school should have a curriculum and pedagogy that not only resonate with the dominant culture of the school but also are inclusive of other cultures that may be represented. This was not the case in Tiara's own K-12 school experiences.

She was a student in inner city schools that were nearly 100% Black. The curriculum? White-oriented. The teachers? Nearly all White. In her entire K-12 student life, forty of her teachers were White and seven were Black. She relates that she was frustrated with the White-dominated curriculum taught by mostly White teachers until the month of February. February was and is the traditional month for Black history.

In her dissertation, Tiara wrote that in February her school experiences were happy ones because books and materials resonated with her. She relates it this way:

February was the month I read the most . . . February was the month that the "Black" books were put out in our classroom libraries. February was when I was able to read about characters who not only looked like me but also had many of the same experiences as me growing up in the inner city. In February, I was allowed to embrace my culture and heritage. February was the month that my white fellow students were able to learn something about me and my people . . . In February, I felt that my white teachers wanted to learn about me and who I was as a Black person growing up in America. During February, I felt like I mattered.[12]

When March arrived Tiara felt that her culture was once again "pushed back deep into the classroom closet."[13] She continued to express her frustration: "the same white teachers who were so 'WOKE' during the month of February suddenly became 'sleep' and forgot (or ignored) the culturally diverse student learners who were in front of them."[14]

Twenty years later, Tiara found herself on the other side of the teacher's desk. Her role among her colleagues was also different. As the only Black person out of thirty-four classroom teachers, she was in a position to influence others. When February rolled around, she was the one who was sought to provide multicultural ideas and materials to the other teachers for Black history month. In many ways, this role frustrated her. She felt that the White teachers relied on her to plan and distribute resources for Black History Month because, as she states, "the Black teacher got it."[15]

Multicultural Professional Development

It was this frustration and passion that led her to choose a topic and title for her doctoral dissertation at Saint Joseph's University: "Stay Woke: Using Professional Development to Increase White Elementary Teachers' Sense of Self-efficacy in Using Multicultural Literature Inside of the Classroom." To begin her research, she developed and gave a survey to all of the teachers. Out of thirty-four teachers, twenty-three responded.

Data from the survey revealed that only 21 percent of participants had received some type of training using multicultural literature resources inside of their classroom. This survey also showed that 73 percent of the participants were not confident and 91 percent of the participants were not comfortable with using multicultural literature. Tiara's next step was to design five weeks of professional development for all of the twenty-three respondents.

The professional development sessions were designed to explore African American, Native American, Asian American, and Latino literature. Sessions were held weekly and covered these main topics: definitions of multiculturalism and multicultural literature; power and privilege;

unpacking Whiteness; multicultural picture books; cultural authenticity; and development of an action plan. From the twenty-three participants, she chose four to be part of in-depth pre- and post-interviews that gave rich perspectives to the weekly writing prompts and surveys given to all of the twenty-three participants.

The professional development sessions were lively with rich dialogue based on resources that Tiara provided. Among these resources were twenty-eight different books and connections to sixteen different websites. A listing of these can be found in her dissertation which is cataloged at ProQuest. The in-depth interviews from the four teachers gave added depth and valuable feedback to the weekly sessions.

A survey given at the conclusion of the professional development sessions found that all twenty-three teachers who participated "strongly agreed" or "agreed" that the professional development sessions prepared them to teach multicultural literature in a multicultural classroom.[16] In the conclusion of her dissertation, Tiara wrote "the participants felt that the professional development . . . equipped them with some of the necessary skills needed to be comfortable and confident with incorporating multicultural literature inside of their classrooms."[17]

Tiara demonstrated a remarkable sense of personal agency when she decided to challenge the way that literature was taught to multicultural students in her school. Her own personal background sensitized her to the alienation that can occur when only White literature is taught to students of different races and cultural backgrounds. In enrolling in a doctoral program and focusing her dissertation on the problem, she revealed her strong qualities as a transformational leader that affected change.

In this example, Tiara's transformational educational leadership qualities and actions can be summarized as follows:

- Mission—she created a greater degree of equity in the teaching of literature to elementary school students;
- Vision—she developed a substantive professional development program that brought rich multicultural resources and teaching/learning strategies to an all-White faculty;
- Community—she created a community of learners wherein all participants felt they were valued and together the community experienced a metamorphosis in experiencing multicultural literature.

The next example of an inspirational person who can be labeled both a transformational leader and a transformational educator is Sr. Henrietta formerly of Cleveland, Ohio.

SISTER HENRIETTA: ANGEL OF MERCY

Sister Henrietta was actually a nurse supervisor at Saint Vincent Charity Hospital in Cleveland. One day it hit her. The strong sense of mission that was beating in her heart was not manifested in her relatively comfortable setting. She left the hospital to work with a priest in the center of one of Cleveland's most impoverished neighborhoods. She wanted to bring her sense of mission to life by using her skills to teach others ways to improve their lives.

Riots and Our Lady of Fatima Mission House

The most serious riots in Cleveland's history began on July 18, 1966. They started in an urban region known as Hough—a two square mile area that went from a predominantly White middle-class neighborhood in 1950 to a predominantly non-White one in 1960.[18] Before the Ohio National Guard was able to restore calm 7 days after the riots began, 4 people had been killed, 30 seriously injured, and nearly 300 arrested. More than 240 fires had turned the area into one that resembled a war zone.

Many people, fearful of their lives, fled Hough following the first gunshots and fires. A sixty-four-year-old nun refused to leave the mission where she worked at East 68th Street and Quimby Avenue. Her name was Sister Henrietta. She was an inspiration to many people in the Hough area because of her charitable work—work that improved the lives of hundreds of distressed children, women, and men. These people were the ones who formed a protective circle around her. It must have been a truly remarkable sight to see this relatively short woman stand tall in her full white habit against the violence that was engulfing the neighborhood.

Sister Henrietta's career was in nursing. She graduated from Canton's Mercy Hospital School of Nursing in 1925. That same year she entered the religious order of the Sisters of Charity of Saint Augustine and took her final vows in 1931. She became a supervisor of nurses and an administrator at Mercy hospital until she left to become director of nursing services at Cleveland's Saint Vincent Charity Hospital in 1962. In 1965 she left the hospital and moved to a humble Hough area parish known as Our Lady of Fatima.

In the mid-1960s, Our Lady of Fatima was more than a local parish serving Catholic families. A large number of Catholics had moved from the area, and Our Lady of Fatima became a social mission to serve the people of Cleveland's worst urban ghetto.

The parish's pastor, Father Albert Koklowsky, was known for his outspoken writings that appeared in the Cleveland diocese's *Catholic Universe*

Bulletin. An example of his passionate voice is found in a quotation from his column entitled "A Voice from the Slums" in which he wrote:

What I have to write is not pleasant, because I live in a ghetto.
Here my people and I move in a nightmare in a festering junkyard.
Ghettos are created by men for the less fortunate, the least lovable.
My ghetto is a creation of the Great Society which has forgotten how to love and how to pity. Here the almighty dollar takes precedence over human dignity.
In the ghetto where I live, the littered, glass-strewn streets separate the trampled, grassless lawns. Dirty papers rustle on the pavement and tumble into corners.
Sidewalks are spotted with stinking mattresses, rusty springs, crumbling furniture. Garbage and rubbish pickups are slow, slow, slow.
There are odors—57 varieties—stomach-flipping stenches. Our backyards are jammed with junk and cans and paper and rats.[19]

Words such as these resonated with Sister Henrietta. Her reason for leaving hospital life was simple. She came to a realization that her antiseptically clean life within a man-made bubble was not the encounter with the world that she read in Christ's gospel message. So she left and joined Father Koklowsky's mission.[20]

One of the major programs that Sister Henrietta started soon after arriving at Our Lady of Fatima was known as Caridad—Spanish for charity and an acronym for Charity and Responsibility in Deed and Duty. Caridad, consisting primarily of Hough area women, organized programs dealing with health care, cleanliness, and disease prevention. It also established food, clothing, and furniture banks for neighborhood residents.

Caridad's constitution echoed and expanded the words of our *Declaration of Independence* by stating that "Our neighbors have the right to life in the mainstream of America, to liberty from debilitating disease and poverty, to the pursuit of happiness with decent education and employment."[21]

Response to Vertical Filing Cabinets

Perhaps the most dramatic project that Sister Henrietta started was known as Famicos. This program, still in existence, was her response to urban high-rise housing developments that she labeled "vertical filing cabinets for people."[22]

Famicos was a very energetic program that involved the men of the neighborhood and revealed Sister Henrietta that was as tough as nails. Slogans symbolizing Famicos's goals were to "make every house a home" and "improve, don't move."[23]

Some of Famicos's projects included providing financial advice and doing house maintenance/improvement work. More important was its home leasing and ownership program. This involved organizing neighborhood men to rebuild houses after Sister Henrietta worked to get them condemned by the city.

After the houses were thoroughly renovated, they were leased to families for low monthly rents that were used to help pay the renovation debts. After the debts were repaid in approximately fifteen years, the family had the option of taking ownership for a nominal cost. As of 1995, approximately 450 houses had been renovated and leased this way.[24] Sister Henrietta was helped greatly in these efforts by the volunteer work of Robert Wolf, a vice president for B.F. Goodrich, who gave up his job to work with the Famicos project.

The effects of this program were amazing to see. Several blocks of well-maintained houses with neat landscaping stood out as an oasis in the midst of 1970s urban blight. The idea of organizing neighborhoods so that residents could be empowered was somewhat unique at this time.

Sister Henrietta's impact in both community-organizing and improving racial relations was recognized by awards that include the Catholic Interracial Council Award, the National Urban Coalition's Distinguished Community Service Award, and the American Jewish Committee's Micah Award. Another great impact of hers, one not recognized by awards or well-known beyond a few individuals, was the inspiration that she gave to a small group of teachers and students from the all-White Normandy High School that was located in the suburb of Parma, Ohio.

Encounter with Students from an All-White Suburb

Normandy High School opened in the fall of 1968. It was the newest and most innovative of Parma's three high schools. The principal, Wesley Gaab, and the assistant principal, Marty Kane, were constantly seeking better ways to make learning come alive for the more than 2,700 students attending the school in the early 1970s. One of the programs that they initiated was called Experience in Free Form Education or EFFE.

Wes Gaab introduced the EFFE idea to approximately 135 Normandy teachers at a faculty meeting in the fall of 1971. It was an ambitious idea that entailed abolishing the entire high school curriculum for one week and replacing it with hands-on courses conducted both at the school and in the greater community. Teachers could develop courses that they had always wanted to teach but could not because of bureaucratic restraints. Once courses were developed and approved, Gaab and Kane developed an entirely new master schedule and opened registration for students.

Some courses were held in the school and consisted of an extensive array of community and business speakers. Many involved extended trips that incorporated weekends and lasted up to nine days. Examples of these included an in-depth study of theatre in New York City and environmental studies of the Mississippi delta in Louisiana. Others utilized regional community resources such as a course on criminal studies that involved lectures from attorneys and visitations to courtrooms as well as prisons.

Four social studies, teachers at Normandy High School developed a course on the city of Cleveland that was designed to provide sociological experiences that students could not get from lectures or textbooks while sitting in their all-White suburban classrooms. This author was one of those teachers. He along with three other teachers and twenty-five students explored the city for five days in unbelievably rich ways.

One of the speakers in Little Italy shocked most of the group when he described how it was possible to fill the area with armed men from the suburbs in case any African Americans tried moving into the neighborhood. This comment set a dramatic backdrop for the most memorable encounter—an in-depth visit with Sister Henrietta in Hough.

None of the students had ever been to an urban ghetto. Few had any previous substantive contact with African Americans. They listened in astonishment as Sister Henrietta opened an unknown world for them.

She described the horror of finding a woman who had been dead for several days being eaten by rats. She described children going to school with different shoes on their left and right feet; children not being ashamed but grateful that they had shoes at all. She told of high rents being charged by slum landlords for apartments in houses that had been subdivided many times. She explained that these same houses had inadequate plumbing and antiquated heating systems. This meant that during winter months many residents were very cold while others within the same house had to open windows to keep from roasting.

After sharing these and other stories Sister Henreitta described her work in founding both Caridad and Famicos. Students accompanied her on walks through the neighborhood and saw the "Spic' n Span" award signs for meeting cleanliness standards proudly displayed in many windows. They visited food and clothing banks, talked with volunteers, and were impressed as they walked by some of Famicos's renovated houses nestled in the urban wasteland.

Most students were somber if not totally silent on their forty-five-minute trip back to their safe suburban school. When they did speak the words came from a confused mix of disbelief and empathy. Eyes had been opened.

Bridges had been built. As the months and years unfolded many of these young adults referred back to the EFFE week as one of the most powerful of their lives.

Sister Henrietta's transformational educational leadership qualities and actions can be summarized as follows:

- Mission—her deep spiritual convictions inspired her to leave a comfortable job in a major urban hospital to combat poverty and racism in one Cleveland's most impoverished neighborhoods;
- Vision—she educated others and helped develop dignified and substantive programs designed to feed, clothe, and house impoverished children and adults;
- Community—she created a strong spiritual community dedicated to building positive self-esteem among its members thereby creating both physical and spiritual metamorphoses.

The next example of a transformational educational leader is found far removed from the urban ghetto that became Sister Henrietta's home. It is high up in the Andes Mountains of Bolivia.

FATHER ENRIQUE OIZUMI

Father Enrique is a Catholic Jesuit priest whose sense of mission is based upon core spiritual values. He translated these values into a passion for educating all children in Bolivia in the richest ways possible through his leadership of *Fe y Alegria*.[25]

Fe y Alegria and Father Enrique

Fe y Alegria, a Jesuit organization, was begun in Venezuela by Fr. Jose M. Velaz in 1955 and is now a highly respected educational support and leadership organization in ten Latin American countries. It began to organize schools in Bolivia in 1966 and by 2003 more than 260,000 students, approximately 6.5 percent of Bolivian students, were in *Fe y Alegria* schools.

In *Fe y Alegria* schools, teachers and administrators are paid the same meager salary as their colleagues in schools directly run by the government. However, a waiting list exists of government schools wanting to become *Fe y Alegria* ones. In large part, this is because of the extensive professional development provided for teachers that emphasized Jesuit values of *cura personalis* (care of each person) and *magis* (always seeking more for each individual). These core values lead to a strong sense of community.

As the director of *Fe y Alegria*, Father Enrique was responsible for instituting and perpetuating these values. He was a role model for living a simple life dedicated to serving others. He gave up a life of wealth to become a Jesuit. He later gave up a life of relative ease as head of the private Catholic school, Saint Calixto in La Paz, to become a parish priest in a native Aymara parish on the El Alto plain above La Paz.

This author attended a Sunday morning mass led by Father Enrique in El Alto—a plain above La Paz that today has a population of approximately 950,000. This is one of the fastest-growing regions in Bolivia as peasants from rural areas seek what they think may be a better life in an urban environment. This was much more than a Sunday morning mass as it lasted well into the afternoon. It was a rich ceremony—both spiritually and socially. Women came in their native dress of full skirts and Bowler hats whereas men came more simply dressed with many of them bringing instruments such as *flautas* (flutes) and *zamponas* (panpipes).

The mass contained the basic traditional elements of a Catholic mass with many added features such as dancing, presentation of harvest gifts, and prayers to the Virgin Mary as well as Pachamama (mother earth). Following the mass, a festive meal was served potluck style. Those who were able brought food with most attendees trying to contribute something. It was clearly evident that this was a tight community that came together to celebrate simple gifts of life in a festive way. Father Enrique said that it was here that he learned the necessity of blending his beliefs with those of the indigenous population.

University Professors, Father Enrique, and *Yachi Wasi*

Father Enrique's sense of mission based upon core spiritual values was evident upon first meeting him. He translated these values into a passion for educating all children in Bolivia in the richest ways possible. One example is when he invited some professors from Saint Joseph's University in Philadelphia to provide a seminar to educational leaders from throughout Bolivia in the summer (winter in Bolivia) of 2003.

This was the reason this author first met him. He and two colleagues from Saint Joseph's went to Bolivia to teach a two-week seminar to thirty-five school leaders in the city of Cochabamba, located high in the Andes Mountains. Meeting Enrique was one thing—getting to really know him was another matter.

This happened when we traveled with him to see some of the flagship *Fe y Alegria* schools known by their Quecha word *Yachi Wasi*. The word literally means House of Learning, and that is what they are. These elementary and secondary schools were designed to serve some of indigenous Aymara, Quechua, and Guarini who made up more than half of Bolivia's eight million people. The schools were created to house and educate students where the road ended. To get to these schools, we had to drive on many dry creek beds as the road truly did abruptly end.

Students often had to walk ten miles or more to get to their schools. Being nearly impossible to do on a daily basis, they would walk to school on Monday mornings and return to their homes on Friday afternoons. One site that we visited was the elementary school known as the *Rodeo Yachi Wasi*. Another was the *Tata Estaban Yachi Wasi* secondary school. The sense of community permeating *Fe Y Alegria* schools was evident in both schools but was particularly strong at the *Tata Estaban Yachi Wasi*.

Here approximately 160 high school students literally ran the school. In addition to attending classes, each student had daily chores that included cleaning communal bathrooms, preparing/serving meals, and maintaining school buildings. Students appeared to be eager to learn and were highly respectful of each other. These are some of the attributes that apparently grew from a strong commitment that these schools had in developing the importance of "community" as opposed to a global commercialism that stressed individual competition and the cult of self.

Seminar in Cochabamba

This sense of community demonstrated at the *Tata Estaban Yachi Wasi* was also evident during the two-week seminar offered by Saint Joseph's professors for *Fe y Alegria* school leaders. The seminar focused on strategic planning, curriculum development, and leadership. It consisted of group analyses of common readings, case studies, role-playing activities, and designing as well as presentation of group projects.

These projects utilized technology and used the internet to an extremely high degree. This was a powerful lesson for Saint Joseph's professors who had wrongly equated the poverty evident in Bolivia with backwardness. Another amazing lesson learned was the impressive communal attitude and work ethic that participants brought to the seminar.

It was obvious from the beginning that the North American emphasis on individual competition and achievement was not the norm for this group. Leadership flowed effortlessly from person to person with no individual domination. Participants used breaks and worked late into the evenings reading cooperatively in groups and raising questions about materials prior to seminar sessions. Cooperation was especially strong during group presentations. These were always followed by rousing rounds of applause.

This cooperative spirit carried over into activities apart from the seminar. We lived together in simple quarters sharing communal bathrooms and taking meals in common dining facilities. Participants took upon themselves preparation for chapel services each afternoon that included music, group singing, and spiritual reflections. As we had no TV or radio, participants planned entertainment each evening that consisted of social games, singing, and dancing.

The setting for the seminar was a school that had formerly been used to board promising students of indigent miners from Potosi. It then became a day school for approximately 175 students from Cochabamba. Students were heavily involved in running the school, and between classes, they cleaned the communal bathrooms, swept walkways, did landscape work, and ran the small office. In addition to these chores, they earned money for the school by preparing meals and renting out the former sleeping facilities to organizations such as *Fey y Alegria*.

One evening, students from the school provided musical entertainment for us. Dressed in colorful Aymara and Quechua clothing, students—proudly aware of their indigenous cultures—led us through traditional dances while playing *flautas* (flutes) and *zamponas* (panpipes) to the beat of large and small drums. The swirl of color, exotic sounds, and circling bodies produced an intoxication that bonded strangers and gave emphasis to the concept of community that permeated this school.

The collaboration between Saint Joseph's University and *Fe y Alegria* helped to define further this sense of community that continues to this day. It is built upon the principles specified by the former Superior General of the Jesuits, Father Pedro Arrupe who stated that "Only by being a man or woman for others does one become fully human."[26] Father Arrupe's words live in Father Enrique's rich contributions to *Fe y Aegria* and to education in both Bolivia and Philadelphia.

Father Enrique Oizumi is a true transformational educational leader whose qualities and actions can be summarized as follows:

- Mission—his deep spiritual values as a Jesuit defined nearly every aspect of his life;
- Vision—his deep sense of mission was manifested through his leadership of *Fe y Alegria* and his reaching out to others in North America to give continuous life to that organization;
- Community—whether leading mass on the plains of El Alto or dancing with professors from Saint Joseph's University, he built a strong community wherever he went thereby creating spiritual metamorphoses.

The next example of a transformational educational leader is of a remarkably bright and talented teacher and coordinator of social studies in Parma,

Ohio—Cleveland's largest suburb. Leonard Lang: Changing a Curriculum to Better Understand Crucial World Issues

Leonard Lang literally turned the conceptualization and teaching of secondary social studies upside down through his leadership that revolutionized a tired, staid curriculum that by its very nature resisted change.

The American social revolution of the late 1960s was a time for deep questioning. Issues of war and peace, racial relations, poverty, and environmental concerns were among the serious topics debated by university intellectuals, writers, religious leaders, and everyday American citizens. Political, social, religious, economic, and educational institutions were confronted by fresh thinkers who challenged historic practices.

Teaching of Social Studies and Survival of our Species

Leonard Lang was known as one of the outstanding educators in the Parma, Ohio, school district.[27] Following his return from a year's study in 1962 as a John Hay Fellow, he was chosen as Parma's district-wide coordinator for secondary social studies. This position meant that he was responsible for selecting, mentoring, and supervising approximately seventy-five teachers who were divided among six junior and three senior high schools. It was in creating a community of learners to change an outmoded curriculum that Leonard demonstrated his skills and sensitivities as a transformational educational leader.

At a meeting of the entire secondary social studies department in the fall of 1969, he raised a very serious concern. As an avid reader of important American magazines—such as *Saturday Review*, *Atlantic Monthly* and *Harper's*—he was troubled by the issues that they were raising regarding the future of our species on earth. He indicated that there were four critical issues that, if not addressed in the near future, could grow into crises and result in the possible elimination of life on earth as we know it.

The four issues that he identified were:

- the possibility of nuclear war and the annihilation of entire nations;
- worldwide racial hatred that manifested itself in ongoing violence;
- overpopulation and the possibility of worldwide hunger;
- environmental waste and damage caused by increasingly rapid consumption of finite natural resources.

Leonard's big question—where in the Parma 7–12 social studies curriculum were these issues addressed? The answer—nowhere.

The Parma schools social-studies curriculum in the late 1960s was typical of that found in most American public schools:

- seventh grade—general world geography;
- eighth grade—U.S. history with some emphasis on specific state history;
- ninth grade—civics (one semester);
- tenth grade—world history (for college-bound students);
- eleventh grade—U.S. history (required for all students);
- twelfth grade—U.S. government (one-semester, required for all students);
- required elective one semester (sociology, psychology, economics) for noncollege-bound students.

The high school curriculum leveled the required courses. This meant that advanced students were assigned to honors or advanced placement courses, challenged students were in basic classes and most students were in regular sections.

The customary pedagogy for all courses was teacher-lecture based upon commonly adopted textbooks. For yearlong courses, these texts usually consisted of thirty-six chapters (the number of weeks in the school year), and teachers were expected to cover approximately one chapter per week. These texts were chosen from national publishers which meant that they were written to be accepted in diverse parts of the country.

The power exerted by state school boards and departments of education in single adoption states such as Texas or California was enormous in dictating the subject matter of the books. This meant that the content was usually noncontroversial, safe and—in one word—bland. Teacher lectures were supplemented with worksheets that were designed to prepare students for recall answers on weekly quizzes and unit tests that usually consisted of multiple-choice, true/false, and fill-in-the-blank questions.

Learning seldom moved beyond the lowest levels of information gathering, and there were a few analysis, synthesis, or evaluation activities in courses other than honors or advanced placement. The history courses, for example, emphasized chronologies while ignoring the interplay between social, economic, political, geographical, and psychological forces that are important for students to develop critical understandings of historical issues and trends.

Government classes stressed surface knowledge of legislative, executive, and judicial processes outlined in our national and state constitutions without exploring real political processes in action. It was no wonder that teachers often complained of students sleeping in the class—even with their eyes wide open.

Alternatives to Traditional Social Studies

Leonard Lang proposed that alternatives to the traditional curriculum be explored to make courses more meaningful for students as well as address the serious issues that he had identified for the teachers. Teachers were generally enthusiastic but wondered if examining the traditional curriculum would involve more than simply choosing a new edition of a threadbare textbook. Lang assured them that he had commitments from the district's curriculum director and superintendent for them to develop a model secondary social studies curriculum.

They were to begin with blank paper and dream as they developed an ideal. With these assurances, many teachers volunteered to be on an exploratory committee that developed a process that became a model for curriculum development that was eventually adopted by other departments in the district and elsewhere.

The model used for curriculum development began by examining expectations that social studies educators had for students upon their graduation from the district. What was the basic knowledge expected of students for them to be successful in college or in their chosen career? What were the basic skills and attitudes necessary for them to become productive and self-actualizing the United States and world citizens?

The next step was to examine the existing K-12 curriculum and determine how successful it was in achieving the expectations. This entailed teachers visiting not only different classes within their own buildings but also classes at all grade levels. For most of the teachers, these visits were a first, and many eyes were opened as high school teachers visited elementary and junior high classrooms while junior high teachers visited the high school and elementary classes. From these visits, teachers gained district-wide perspectives and perceptions that were later shared at several district-wide meetings.

These visitations produced many ideas and questions that prompted a study of national social studies curricula. Information for this study was gathered from the National Council of Social Studies, the state department of education, and a broad range of school districts. These studies were compiled and discussed by teachers at both building level and district-wide meetings. Following the study phase, each building chose representatives to be part of a district committee whose purpose was to design a philosophy of social studies education.

In the early winter of 1970, a group of approximately thirty secondary social studies teachers and administrators met for a three-day/two-night retreat at Ohio's Punderson State Park. Their purpose, articulated by Lang, was to develop a new philosophy of social studies education. He led them through invigorating intellectual and emotional experiences. Individuals dialogued, discussed, argued, and eventually agreed upon a one-paragraph philosophy that encompassed not only traditional views regarding the significance of learning history and civics but also the importance of substantively addressing social justice ideals from world perspectives.

This committee also determined that survey texts, lectures, and low-level objective tests should, for the most part, be eliminated and replaced with a variety of learning materials and rich assessments. These included relevant paperback books, films, simulations, field experiences, and oral as well as written assessments of the curriculum's goals and objectives.

This new philosophy was presented to all of the secondary social studies teachers where it was, again, discussed in great detail at building-level meetings. After some additional modifications were made, it was voted upon and became the social studies educational philosophy. The next step was to identify course structures that would implement the philosophy. This meant specifying grade levels, courses, goals, objectives, activities, and assessments.

Based upon the Punderson philosophy, it was decided to increase the student's choice in the required courses. The biggest change gave them an option to the yearlong survey course in U.S. history and the semester course in government. This option consisted of students selecting from nineteen different courses that were offered in nine-week modules.

Examples of nine-week courses included "Black History," "Colonial America," "Crisis in Urban American Life," "Dissent and Democracy," "Law in American Society," "Minority Struggle," "Presidential Power," "War and Peace," and "Worlds in the Making." Changes were also made in the seventh-, eighth-, and ninth-grade offerings as well as in the world history survey course as new materials that emphasized the higher order thinking skills were introduced.

All of the district's secondary social studies courses were rewritten to reflect both the content and pedagogy of the Punderson philosophy. This was done by teams of teachers who filled rooms with various types of books and other learning materials. Lang believed that students and their teachers rather than authoritative texts from outside sources should be at the center of the educational process.

Leonard Lang's perspective of viewing teachers in this highly professional way was stimulating and it encouraged teachers to respond positively to the demands made upon them by the new curriculum. After extensive professional development, the new curriculum went into effect in the fall of 1970. The response from both students and teachers was very positive. It was assessed at the end of the 1971 school year, and course guides were rewritten the following summer based upon those assessments. This curriculum process proved to be so successful that it was adopted by several other departments not only in this district but in many surrounding ones as well.

The Parma social studies curriculum lasted for several years until it was undone by conservative curriculum forces similar to those whose voices dominated the1983 *Nation at Risk* taskforce publication. These same forces are evident today in the high-stakes testing movement.

The Parma experiment had both its advocates and its critics. What was clear to both is that for a period of time high school students were encouraged to be in greater control of their own learning. They responded by taking more courses in social studies than were required for graduation.

Teachers were excited by the new courses and classroom learning went from fact-recall to analysis, synthesis, and evaluation of major historical, sociological, governmental, and social justice issues. Leonard Lang's questions regarding where the world crises issues of racial hatred, nuclear war, overpopulation, and destruction of the environment were found in the curriculum had been answered. It was Parma's social studies curriculum.

Leonard Lang was successful in creating a community of learners whose common mission was the education of future citizens and whose vision was making social studies education come alive by addressing serious social justice issues before they became species-threatening crises. For these reasons, he truly was a transformational leader whose qualities and actions can be summarized as follows:

- Mission—his deep sense of social justice and issues of equity revealed a strong, spiritual sense of mission;
- Vision—his sense of mission permeated his thinking and leadership which led to a vision of a new social studies curriculum that manifested issues of social justice and equity;
- Community—his leadership in developing the Punderson philosophy created a vital sense of community that was able to change an outmoded curriculum and led to true metamorphoses in social studies education.

The next case study is of a woman who vitalized a community of learners through a common mission and lofty vision. Her name is Sister Rosemary Hocevar—a name recognized and respected throughout the Cleveland area for her strong leadership and compassionate spirit.[28] She represents the qualities of a true transformational educational leader—mission, vision, and community.

SISTER ROSEMARY HOCEVAR

Sister Rosemary was the principal of Villa Angela Academy, a respected girls' high school on Cleveland's east side not far from Euclid Beach amusement park. The school was a traditional Catholic high school until Sister Rosemary led the teachers, students, parents, and alumni through a process that redefined the school's mission and institutionalize it into a new building. The expression that captured the community's inspired philosophy was "Touching Tomorrow Together."

Sister Rosemary Hocevar and "Touching Tomorrow Together"

Founded in 1878 by a religious order known as the Order of Saint Ursula (OSU), Villa Angela Academy was one of the oldest Catholic schools in the Cleveland diocese. The order's all-women high school was housed in a fortress-like building that by the late 1960s was literally crumbling. The Cleveland diocese raised funds in the 1960s to build new Catholic high schools. Villa Angela was one of these. The Ursuline community who ran the school hired innovative architect Richard Fleischman to design it. At one of their initial meetings with him, the sisters learned a very important lesson.

He would not begin the design process until they were able to express a commonly held educational philosophy that grew from their mission of Catholic education. Fleischman believed that if the building was to reinforce this mission then the design needed to be a living testament to their beliefs—and it truly needed to belong to them.

The school's principal Sister Rosemary clearly heard his message. The date for the proposed groundbreaking was delayed for more than one year during which she created a community of learners by engaging students, faculty, parents, and alumni in numerous conversations. These were intended to challenge their beliefs and build common understandings. At the end of the year, they published a pamphlet entitled "Touching Tomorrow Together" that contained their educational philosophy as well as a program and pedagogy to manifest it.

The educational program stressed Christian social justice values and high academic standards. These standards were to be achieved through an interdisciplinary curriculum that combined math with science and English with social studies. Performing/visual arts, foreign languages, business, and physical education were also prominently featured.

Helping others was an expectation for all students, and during their sophomore year, every young woman participated for a full year in various community service projects. The entire school program was facilitated by a close relationship between faculty and students as teachers became advisors for approximately 25 ninth graders and remained with them for four years.

A Mission realized in a New Villa Angela

Once "Touching Tomorrow Together" had been adopted by the faculty, representatives of the teachers, students, parents, and alumni held regular meetings with Fleischman to design the new school. They quickly learned that every building represents a philosophy and that a school can be much more than a place to house faculty and students.

Fleishman insisted that their school becomes one that personified their deepest beliefs. They also learned that Fleishman was both a gifted artist and a technician. Being both, his approach to architectural design was that it should embody both artistic and practical elements. In describing his approach to design, Fleishman wrote "good architecture maintains a consistent quality and image, which represent not only a network of artistic and functional spaces, but a powerful commitment to great design."[29]

The design process itself was a creative experience for members of the community as they debated different plans that would bring their philosophy to life. The experience was also an aesthetic one as they learned from Fleishman ways that shapes, colors, and materials could combine to form different environments and feelings. Creating the design helped form their community and caused them to transcend the ordinary. Sister Rosemary stated that going through this process was "the time of my life."[30] The resulting building captured their philosophy and translated it into an aesthetic, organic, living structure.

At the center of the school was a large multileveled rectangular-shaped media center which proclaimed to all that academic learning was of paramount importance. On the lower level of the media center was the library. Next to the media center, at the heart of the school, was a chapel with an altar made from a large tree taken from the grounds of the original school. By placing the chapel adjacent to the media center, the design stressed that spirituality was at the core of academic pursuits.

On the main level, surrounding the media center, were semi-open academic classrooms which housed the interdisciplinary curriculum. Floating above these and flowing into the upper portions of the media center were student lockers, commons, and work areas. These were next to open-spaced teacher carrels. Bringing students and teachers together in this manner facilitated ongoing contact and personalized each student's education. The auditorium/large group instruction room, cafeteria, gymnasium, art, and music areas were adjacent to the media center/academic core.

When the school opened in 1972, the faculty, students, and alumni were excited with the final product and recognized that theirs was a unique learning space. The school's design received praise from the community and was recognized by the Greater Cleveland Growth Association with a Certificate of Merit in 1973. The media center design received an Award of Merit in 1974 from the American Institute of Architects.

The history of this unique building took a sad turn for educators in 1988 when the Diocese of Cleveland announced that because of declining enrollments Villa Angela would be merged with Saint Joseph's, a Catholic boys high school. Today the school is known as Villa Angela-Saint Joseph's High School and occupies the former Saint Joseph's High School building on Lake

Shore Boulevard in Cleveland. What was Villa Angela High School is now the Memorial Nottingham Branch of the Cleveland Public Library system.

Sister Rosemary, now retired, was an associate professor of educational administration and later an administrator at Ursuline College in Pepper Pike, Ohio. After leaving Villa Angela in 1976 she was a coordinator of secondary education for the Diocese of Cleveland where she remained until 1985 when she went to Kent State to work on her PhD in educational administration. She became the director of the educational administration program at Ursuline in 1989. She is currently retired at the Regina Health Center in Richfield, Ohio.

Over the years Sister Rosemary served on many boards and was a president of the National Catholic Education Association's Secondary School Executive Committee from 2006 to 2009. She served on more than thirty North Central Association evaluation teams in the greater Cleveland area. Of the numerous awards that Sister Rosemary has received, she is most proud of being inducted into the Villa Angela-Saint Joseph's Hall of Fame in 1995. In 2011, she received the Michael Guerra Leadership Award by the National Education Association for an educator whose impact on Catholic secondary schools has a lasting impact.

Of all the outstanding work that she did, she recalls her years at Villa Angela as the highlight of her career. She is truly a transformational leader whose qualities and actions can be summarized as follows:

- Mission—she has a deep sense of mission based upon a spiritual faith that recognizes the important social justice values of charity and service to others;
- Vision—her sense of mission was manifested in the vision that she and members of her community had for a new building that reflected high educational standards and deep social justice values;
- Community—she led the teachers, alumni, parents, and students in designing a school whose essence was captured in "Touching Tomorrow Together."

The next example of a transformational educational leader is of a man who went from being a highly recognized social worker, elementary principal, and pupil personnel director in a nationally known public school system to becoming superintendent of a small, struggling suburban district.

JACK THOMAS

Jack Thomas's belief in the basic principle that an entire community was responsible for providing its future citizens with a quality education was unwavering. He turned a group of teachers, parents, students, and citizens into a community of advocates for children who shared his passion for public education. These believers campaigned against great odds to pass a bond issue that added badly needed facilities for a distressed school district. His transformational leadership combated indifference, selfishness, and class distinctions based on property wealth that often leads to bitterness and hatred.

Jack Thomas: Split Community = Split Sessions

Jack Thomas became superintendent of the North Royalton School District located in the outer ring of Cleveland's suburbs in 1972.[31] He inherited a serious problem of overcrowding as building growth had not kept pace with the increase in student population. Ohio requires local voter approval for building construction bonds as the state does not, as a general rule, provide building funds.

The district had tried gaining that approval from voters several times and failed. Faced with a difficult dilemma, the district resorted to scheduling sixth, seventh, and eighth graders in the middle school to double or split sessions. This meant that the building was used from 6:00 a.m. until 6:30 p.m. Sixth graders and one-half of the seventh attended classes from 6:00 a.m. until noon. The eighth graders and the other half of the seventh attended from 12:30 until 6:30 p.m.

While this arrangement met the instructional hours required by the state, it was anything but ideal. Most of the students in the district were transported on busses, and parents complained of the great inconveniences associated with either early or late times. If both parents were working, they had to be concerned with extended day-care issues. Teachers had little sense of a home base or professional community. They were required to make most of their instructional materials portable so that they could be bundled and taken home at the end of their session.

The biggest impact fell upon the students' educational program. There was little time for any education beyond the basics which often had to be taught during times when students would normally be at home or, perhaps, playing with their friends. Fundamental issues, such as building maintenance, strained the staff's resources to provide even rudimentary services. The matter of cafeteria service for lunches was solved simply—it was eliminated.

The inevitable outcry over split sessions from parents, students, and teachers brought them into sharp conflict with the community's old-timers who did not want to pay increased taxes and see changes in their community. It was in resolving this conflict that Jack Thomas proved to be a transformational leader.

CARE and a New School Plan

Ohio law prohibits the expenditure of public funds to promote bond issues or operating levies, so Jack formed a committee of interested parents and citizens that named itself CARE (Concerned About Royalton Education). Their purpose was to raise funds and campaign for a new bond issue. Thomas transformed this committee into community advocates for children who campaigned to pass a new bond issue. Part of the campaign was to explain the proposed building plans with the aid of one of their members who was also a local architect.

Previous plans for an additional bond issue had called for the construction of a new high school. As these had been defeated several times, the committee suggested a very different plan. It recommended, instead, a major addition to the high school that included some classrooms, but also offered a scheme of shared spaces that would minimize costs and maximize benefits.

These shared spaces consisted of a new media center as well as art, music, and physical education facilities. The plan called for a reorganization of students with the eighth grade moving from the middle school to a wing of classrooms at the high school where they would share the common facilities. The plan seemed workable to the committee. The question was whether or not the citizens would vote for the bonds to construct the project.

Jack Thomas inspired committee members to work tirelessly in campaigning for the bond issue. Members spent many evenings, Saturdays, and Sundays going door-to-door to explain the crisis facing the district and the plan to resolve it. It was a cold, rainy, November election day in 1974 when voters went to the polls. Many predicted that the weather would hurt the bond issue's chances. The prediction was wrong. The issue narrowly passed. Several hundred people assembled in the high school cafeteria that evening to hear of the results. After victory became clear, Jack entered the room and was greeted as a hero with a loud cheer.

Jack Thomas is a true transformational educational leader whose actions can be summarized as follows:

- Mission—his strong passion and belief in public education became the greater community's common mission;
- Vision—the common mission to provide equitable education for all students was crystallized in a vision for new facilities that eliminated split sessions;
- Community—he created a metamorphosis and a different sense of community that combated indifference and selfishness that can lead to class distinctions and hatred.

The final case study of a transformational educational leader who exemplifies the key elements of mission, vision, and community is that of Jane Golden whose inspiration and leadership has made Philadelphia's mural arts project (Mural Arts Philadelphia) the largest public arts program in the nation.[32]

JANE GOLDEN

In 1977 Jane Golden, a graduate who majored in fine arts and political science at Stanford, moved to the Los Angeles area wondering what she could do with a BA in art. She learned of grants sponsored by the City Wide Mural Project and something inside her clicked. Even though the deadline had passed, she applied for a grant and with persistence eventually received one. At that time it would have been almost unbelievable that forty-one years later (2018) she would be the executive director of Mural Arts Philadelphia which over the years has created more than 3,800 murals making Philadelphia the "world's largest outdoor art gallery."[33]

Artist and Social Activist

Jane Golden's journey to Philadelphia began in 1984 when she was hired to be a field representative in Philadelphia's Anti-Graffiti Network. Here she was able to combine her two university majors—art and political science—to work with "kids from tough neighborhoods"[34] and get them to exchange their cans of spray paint for artists' brushes as they painted murals on public buildings. Jane described her social activism combined with artistry at a special seminar at Saint Joseph's University in 2017.

Tuesday, November 14, 2017. It could have been just another Tuesday evening of classes for approximately seventy-five Saint Joseph's University graduate and doctoral students in the educational leadership department. Instead, the department chair, Encarna Rodriguez, had arranged for Jane Golden to be a guest speaker.

The large seminar room was alive with the usual cell phone checking and texting, chattering and laughing among classmates, and general shuffling and buzzing until Jane started to speak. Things gradually quieted down—and then the magical pin-drop moment. Jane captivated this collection of educators for more than one-and-a-half hours as she told her story: life dreams almost derailed because of her continuous bouts with lupus, passion for social justice manifested in creating communities by building bridges in neighborhoods that defined the term social divide and a passionate belief in pubic pedagogy brought alive through the arts.[35]

In short, it was anything but just another Tuesday evening of classes. Not an educator by training, Jane's story proved that she is a true educator of the highest caliber. Indeed, she is a transformational educator leading others in creating communities based upon principles of social justice and equity for everyone.

Jane's love of mural painting combined with her views on social justice came together and became a powerful force. She wrote:

> Murals have this kind of personal impact. They engage you, stir questions, make you see things in new ways. I don't know if it is their intense color, imposing size, or symbolic power, but they seem to be imbued with a mysterious energy that radiates outward, touching everyone who sees them.[36]

The Philadelphia program moved beyond graffiti prevention, and Jane began to coordinate with various groups in creating murals that would unite groups into communities "touching everyone who sees them." Nowhere is this more powerfully demonstrated than in the Grays Ferry Peace wall.

Grays Ferry Peace Wall: Interlocking Hands

Grays Ferry is a Philadelphia neighborhood that went through a transition during the 1960s when White families began fleeing both the neighborhood and the city. The riots of the early 1970s deepened a racial divide where "you learned quickly around here where you belonged and where you didn't."[37]

Lillian Ray, a Black community activist from the area, and Jane Golden, an outsider White woman, shared a similar dream of creating a mural that could help bridge the Grays Ferry divide which was drawing national attention. They believed that a mural would help heal the ravaged community. Skeptics abounded when they went house to house and were greeted with slammed doors and semi-polite silence.

Then in 1997, a brawl between Black and White men began a racial confrontation that eventually ended in the death of a White teen. This series of events seemed to be the catalyst that brought leaders from both sides of the divide to the realization that something needed to be done. Enter, again, Jane and Lillian. Lillian was now the head of an organization calling itself Grays Ferry United. Resistance to a mural project still existed, but this organization refused to be deterred and organized meetings to explore the idea further. Eventually, with Jane's help, several ideas for a mural symbolic of unity for all Grays Ferry people were discussed.

One design rose above the others. It was decided that interlocking hands was the most sensitive and compelling concept as it seemed to describe to those both inside and outside of the neighborhood what peace meant. Jane directed the project which began with photographing several residents' hands. These eventually became the basis of the mural.

It is truly inspirational to see eleven hands touching one another in a pose similar to a basketball team's interlocking hands during a huddle. Here we see a mix of warm skin colors; some nails semi-painted, some broken; one hand hosting rings on two fingers, and one wrist exposing the cuff of a white shirt and blue coat jacket.

Indeed, here is found diversity and the seeds for a sense of community captured on a large visual approximately two-stories tall—a constant reminder of harmony and peace to those not only in the Grays Ferry neighborhood but those across the city Next to the mural on a painted scroll approximately the size of a five-by-six-foot fence are painted the words "Blessed are the peacemakers: for they shall be called the children of God."[38] Amen.

One of the most unusual and powerful of the various mural projects that Jane Golden directed is one which has been made into a video titled "Concrete, Steel, and Paint."[39] This video describes the development of a project that brought together prisoners and those who had suffered from similar crimes to design and paint a mural that captured their deep emotions.

The site of the former Graterford State Correctional Institution is located on the outskirts of Philadelphia where in 2009 it housed approximately 3,400 prisoners. It was a maximum-security facility, and many of its inmates had been convicted of the most serious crimes. Graterford was replaced in 2018 by a new 350 million dollar facility, the SCI Phoenix Prison. It was in 2009, however, that some of the prisoners at Graterford viewed the video *Concrete, Steel and Paint* and saw themselves as participants in a unique mural arts project

These participants had been regularly involved in art classes offered at the prison. Some had heard of Mural Arts Philadelphia and wondered if they could be involved in designing and painting a mural as a way of helping to reconcile their serious crimes with the community. They wanted to give something back and thought that this was one way of showing remorse. A contact was made with Jane Golden, and she arranged for a meeting with them.

Skeptical at first she began to see value in the idea of bridging the sharp divide between the prison and the greater community through a mural arts project. Opening a small crack in the prison walls might bring some healing for prisoners as well as some members of the community. Before agreeing to proceed, she insisted upon one condition: the project could not include just the prisoners; it also had to include some families and individuals who were victims of crimes similar to the ones that the prisoners had committed.

This condition was more easily stated than accomplished. Relatives of victims carried deep wounds and were not certain that they wanted to meet with prisoners. Prisoners were leery of meeting individuals face-to-face who were severely pained by crimes similar to theirs. Despite the hesitancy, a meeting was eventually held between the two groups. It went better than many feared. There was an initial contact and soon some conversations began to flow.

After several meetings, the concept hit a snag over the design of the mural. It was finally resolved when the decision was made to do two murals to be positioned close to each other so as to show the similarities and differences of varied perspectives. The video, including images of the murals, is available for viewing on the internet at https://www.newday.com/film/concrete-steel-paint.

This project is a potent testimony of the power of art to open dialogue and present new perspectives to participants. As Valerie Keller has written,

> The project challenges both sides to recognize and respect each other's essential humanity and worth—a small, but significant step toward a more healing and restorative form of justice. In telling this story, the film raises important questions about crime, justice and reconciliation—and dramatically illustrates the power of art as a catalyst to facilitate dialogue about these difficult issues.[40]

Simply put, engagement with works of art can change individuals and entire communities. Her passion for bringing arts into everyday life and turning blank walls into imaginative artworks is unique. Jane's strong sense of social justice distinguishes her as a transformational educational leader who is making a positive difference in the lives of thousands of Philadelphians. She epitomizes the key characteristics of a transformational educational leader:

- Mission—her deeply held mission is a passion for the arts and their ability to address issues of social justice;
- Vision—her sense of mission is manifested in a vision that became Mural Arts Philadelphia;
- Community—her sense of mission and vision helped create strong communities among the artists and staff members associated with the various projects as well as the communities with which they are associated.

Summary: Lessons Learned

- Each of the examples presented in this chapter exemplifies in a unique way the central concepts of transformational educational leadership—mission, vision, and community.
- Each of these educators combated hatred or confronted the elements that often lead to hatred—ignorance, indifference, or prejudice.

- Each of them did this by creating a sense of community with a social justice mission that enabled it to achieve a vision that grew from the common mission.
- Each of these transformational educational leaders caused a metamorphosis in their particular situation that lifted the community to a higher plane.

These examples, as well as the others in this book, are inspiring leaders. Many of them combated ignorance and caused those around them to open their eyes and become sensitive to socially unjust situations. Some of them combated intolerance and prejudice. All of them, in one way or another, combated hatred. They are among transformational educators who are leaders for social justice and the recognized equality of all individuals.

NOTES

1. Terrance Furin, "Greatest Teachers" (excerpt), unpublished poem.
2. Comments made by outgoing superintendent Roy Claypool to incoming superintendent Terrance Furin during an introductory meeting in June, 1990.
3. Michael Wall, "Coming into it, #9 of 16: Teaching, year 1: post 671," *Every Good Morning*, http://www.mikewallteacher.com (accessed September 23, 2021).
4. Ibid.
5. Michael Wall, "Coming into it, #8 of 16: Beginning as a teacher: post 670," *Every Good Morning*, http://www.mikewallteacher.com/coming-into-it-3-of-post-670.html (accessed September 24, 2021).
6. Ibid.
7. The professional development course is described in chapter 4, "Combating Neo-Nazi Hate Group."
8. Michael wall, "Poetry, again: Post 716," *Every Good Morning*, http://www.mikewallteacher.com/poetry-again-post-716.html (accessed September 25, 2021).
9. Michael Wall, "Inishmore," *History, 50 Poems* (unpublished), 15.
10. "Fast Facts," The school District of Philadelphia, https://www.philasd.org/fast-facts/ (accessed September 28, 2021).
11. Future Ready PA Index, "Green Woods CS," https://futurereadypa.org/School/FastFacts?id=0441220191502391721802540252331210190552501382 45 (accessed September 28, 2021).
12. Tiara Grymes, *Stay Woke: Using Professional Development to Increase White Elementary Teachers' Sense of Self-efficacy in Using Multicultural Literature Inside of the Classroom*, https://www.proquest.com/results/51C406DA957D4FE7PQ/1?accountid=14071, 2.
13. Ibid.
14. Ibid.
15. Ibid., 3.
16. Ibid., 60

17. Ibid., 92.

18. The *Encyclopedia of Cleveland History*, maintained by Case Western Reserve University, claims that 5% of the Hough area was non-white in 1950 and that in 1960 this number had grown to 74%. See http://ech.case.edu/ech-cgi/article.pl?id=H6 as well as http://ech.case.edu/ech-cgi/article.pl?id=HR3 for a brief history and description of the Hough area and the riots that began in July, 1966. A thesis entitled *The Hough Riots* written by Marc Lackritz provides a more detailed account of the riots. It can be found at http://www.clevelandmemory.org/hough/ (accessed October 10, 2021).

19. Albert Koklowsky, "A voice from the slums," *Catholic Universe Bulletin*, March 19, 1965, 1.

20. Oral description provided by Sister Henreitta to Terrance Furin circa February 15, 1972.

21. Constitution of Caridad provided by an e-mail from Sister Mary Denis (smdm @srsofcharity.org), archivist for the Sisters of Charity of Saint Augustine to Terrance Furin, March 11, 2008.

22. Oral description provided by Sister Henreitta to Terrance Furin circa February 1972.

23. Sister Henrietta's goal for Famicos as provided in an e-mail from Sister Mary Denis (smdm@srsofcharity.org), archivist for the Sisters of Charity of Saint Augustine to Terrance Furin, March 11, 2008.

24. For current information on Famicos see https://www.google.com/search?q=famicos+housing+sproject+sr.+Henrietta&oq=famicos+housing+sproject+sr.+Henrietta&aqs=chrome.69i57j33i10i16ol3.11502j0j15&sourceid=chrome&ie=UTF-8 (accessed October 10, 2021).

25. Author's note: This section on Father Enrique contains only one foot note and is based upon personal knowledge, recollections and notes made during the time that the author worked directly with Father Enrique and *fe y Alegria*.

26. Pedro Arrupe, "Men and women for others," speech given at Valencia Spain, 1973, https://ignatiansolidarity.net/men-and-women-for-others-fr-pedro-arrupe-s-j/ (accessed October 20, 2021). Note the original speech stated only "men for others." This has been modified by *most Jesuit authorities to include "men and women" to make its powerful message applicable for a contemporary Jesuit alumni audience.*

27. This author worked with Leonard Lang for twelve years as a teacher and department chair under his leadership in the Parma school district outside of Cleveland. This account is taken from personal experience and has been verified by his wife after Leonard's death.

28. This author knew Sr. Hocevar well from professional associations in different capacities but especially as members together on many North Central Association evaluation teams.

29. Richard Fleishman, *Spaces to be Shared* (Milan, Italy: l'Arca Edizioni, 1996) front jacket flap.

30. Rosemary Hocevar e-mail to Terrance Furin, January 31, 2008.

31. This author was an assistant superintendent to Jack Tomas for five years being hired by him from the position of chair of the social studies department at Normandy High School We remained colleagues and friends until he died in 2021.

32. "We believe that art ignites change," *Mural Arts Philadelphia*, https://www.muralarts.org/about/ (accessed October 11, 2021).

33. Malerie Yolen-Cohen, "Philadelphia mural arts: The world's largest outdoor art gallery," *Huffpost*, https://www.huffingtonpost.com/malerie-yolencohen/philadelphia-mural-arts-t_b_5092754.html (accessed January 9, 2018).

34. Jane Golden, *The Philadelphia Award*, http://philadelphiaaward.org/jane-golden/ (accessed January 9, 2018).

35. This author is an affiliate professor in the doctoral program at Saint Joseph's University and was present for Jane Golden's presentation.

36. Jane Golden, Robin Rice, and Monica Yant Kinney, *Philadelphia Murals and the Stories they Tell* (Philadelphia: Temple University Press, 2002), 11.

37. Kevin Spicer, lifetime resident of Grays Ferry quoted in Golden, Rice, Kinney, 51.

38. Golden et al. *Philadelphia Murals and the Stories they Tell*, 49.

39. Cindy Burstein and Tony Heriza, directors, video, "Concrete, Steel & Paint," New Day films, available IMBd, http://www.imdb.com/title/tt1684632/ (accessed October 11, 2021).

40. Valerie Keller, "Concrete, steel & paint," *Vimeo*, https://vimeo.com/205242252 (accessed October 11, 2021).

Chapter 8

Becoming Transformational Educational Leaders through Personal Growth

"Leadership springs from *within*. It's about *who I am* as much as what I do."[1]

"Leadership is not a job, not a role one plays at work and then puts aside during the commute home in order to relax and enjoy real life. Rather leadership is the leader's real life."[2]

—Chris Lowney

The first step to becoming a leader is to recognize that leadership must "spring from *within*. (emphasis in original)" That it is "about who I am as much as what I do." Each of the eight leaders presented in the preceding chapter exhibited strong core values that did spring from within. These leaders recognized the importance and grandeur inherent in the soul of each person. This recognition is the foundation of the democratic concept of equality. A democracy's continued vitality relies upon the preservation of this key belief. Educators have a major responsibility in perpetuating the essence of this core value.

Core values grow as they encounter difficult situations that test and strengthen them. It is through this strengthening that educators can become more than educational leaders—they can become transformational ones. Chris Lowney's book, *Heroic Leadership,* provides some important insights that may help us understand the type of transformational leadership that is critical if educational leaders are to engage the challenges facing schools as we move further into the twenty-first century.

LEADERSHIP THAT SPRINGS FROM WITHIN

Four Pillars for Success

The two quotations that begin this chapter are from Lowney's book, and they capture some of the qualities that he believes have enabled the Jesuits, the largest Catholic religious order in the world, to not only survive but also flourish for more than 460 years.[3]

Drawing upon his former life as a Jesuit priest, Lowney presents four "pillars of success" that he considers important in explaining Jesuit endurance: "self-awareness, ingenuity, love, and heroism"[4] (figure 8.1).

He defines them as follows:

- "Self-awareness" is the ability to understand one's strengths, weaknesses, values, and worldviews.
- "Ingenuity" is the talent to innovate and adapt to embrace a changing world.
- "Love" is the capacity to engage others with a positive, loving attitude.
- "Heroism" involves energizing yourself and others through heroic ambitions.

We will focus on the first pillar, "self-awareness," as it is a key to understanding "leadership that springs from within." To understand Lowney's definition more completely, it is helpful to discover the foundation of his core values. This involves learning about the Jesuits, Saint Ignatius, and the Spiritual Exercises.

The Jesuits, Saint Ignatius, and the Spiritual Exercises

The Society of Jesus, known more simply today as the Jesuits, was founded by Ignatius of Loyola in 1534 when, after completing an early version of the

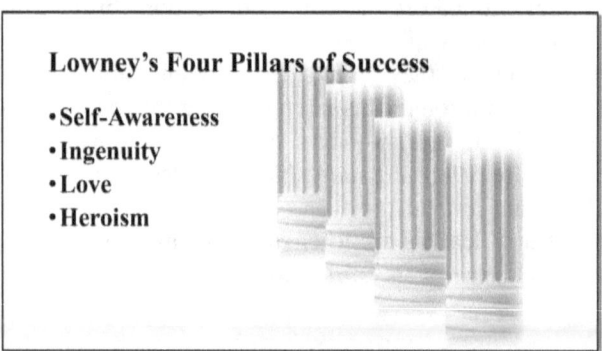

Figure 8.1 Lowney's Four Pillars of Success. *Source*: Author Created.

Spiritual Exercises, six of his followers took vows of poverty, chastity, and obedience. They formed a spiritual community that in 1540 was recognized by Pope Paul III as a Catholic religious order. From the beginning, they determined that their society would not retreat to a mountaintop but would be active in the world serving the poor and downtrodden. Social justice as well as education have become hallmarks associated with their order. Ignatius's conversion from soldier and courtesan to priest and mystic became the foundation for the new order.

Ignatius was born into a relatively wealthy noble family and became an adventurous soldier who enjoyed a free and easy lifestyle at court. This changed after his knee was crushed by a cannonball as he was defending Pamplona from a French invasion. During his yearlong recovery, his vanity caused him to have the bone broken again and reset hoping to lose a limp that had developed. It was also during this recovery that he began to read the few books available to him about the life of Jesus Christ and stories about several different saints.

This began his conversion that deepened through various deep meditations and visions. These became the foundation for the Spiritual Exercises. All Jesuits and many lay individuals make the Exercises. They are designed to take thirty days for completion and require a participant to meditate deeply upon particular experiences and scenes in Jesus's life. There are several annotations of the thirty-day exercises. For example, one known as the Nineteenth Annotation does not require thirty continuous days but replaces it with one hour per day of meditation for twenty-four weeks.

An illustration of a meditation using the Spiritual Exercises might be the following scenario. After reading John's New Testament account of Jesus's call to two of the first disciples, the participant might picture the time of day, feel the weather, breathe in the air and imagine the river or dry land smells, hear the sounds of children, listen to adults talking and then listen to the words of Jesus when he said, "What are you looking for?" The disciples responded, "Where do you live, Rabbi?" Jesus answered, "Come and see."[5]

This scene can be imagined as a plain, powerful, and intimate dialogue. Jesus's invitation for the two to join him at his house for conversation and perhaps some tea, a glass of wine, or a beer both humanizes and spiritualizes this scene.

The Spiritual Exercises are only one way to realize more fully Lowney's first pillar, self-awareness. Another can be found in the simple tagline of the YMCA—Mind, Spirit, Body.

PERSONAL MEDITATION: MIND, SPIRIT, BODY

The YMCA Tagline

Authentic personal meditation takes time and practice. It is not easy for busy educators to find the time or place to meditate daily. It is often the last thing of importance on a plate filled with various must-dos and unforeseen crises. Nonetheless, it is critically important for it to happen regularly if educators want to become transformational leaders. We can learn much from a simple tagline used often by the YMCA.

Familiar to generations of Americans since it was introduced in 1891 is the tagline for the YMCA—Mind, Spirit, Body. This expression advocates for individuals of all ages and genders to live harmonious lives. Educational leaders are usually well-schooled in the mind aspect of this triangle through their own education and required certifications. Many are also familiar with the benefits of regular exercise and good nutrition as a path to greater endurance and well-rounded physical health. To achieve personal harmony, however, they also need to develop the spiritual aspects of the triangle.

When the spiritual aspect of the triangle is nonexistent or weakened, it makes it not only lopsided but also unstable and debilitating. Roger Joslin, in his book, *Running the Spiritual Path*, integrates the physical and spiritual aspects of running. He writes that "the fully actualized human being can neglect neither body nor soul in his striving to become conscious and whole."[6] He writes further, "Remember that we are not merely human beings on a spiritual path, but we are spiritual beings on a human path."[7]

The spiritual side of the triangle can be explored through participation in organized religions. It can also be explored through various forms of meditation such as a vision quest practiced by several Native American tribes, Buddhist meditation, and yoga.

Some Forms of Personal Spiritual Reflection and Meditation

Reflection on particular topics, practices, beliefs, and values usually means that an individual becomes more aware of them. Meditation on the other hand involves deep concentration involving a greater realization of the self in relation to an infinite universe expressed in a starry night sky, a walk in the woods on a wintry day, a sunset over a calm ocean, or the sweetness of a songbird seeking her or his mate.

Perhaps more significantly, meditation can involve a greater realization of the self in relation to other beings. Insights and values gained from regular meditation can become integrated into the very core-being of the participant. There are many variations of meditations. A powerful one is a Native American vision quest.

Vision Quests

Vision quests usually involve individuals preparing their minds and bodies over a period of time to rid themselves of potentially harmful influences. Once they feel ready, they retreat to a private area, oftentimes on top of a mountain, where they fast for one or more days, empty themselves of earthly thoughts, connect with the greater universe, and hope to experience a spiritual awakening. Eagle Man from the Oglala Lakota tribe describes a vision quest this way:

> As each day goes by, the phases of life go through their cycles. At night, the stars come out. Pilades will actually dance for you if you're a vision quester. They light up, almost like a neon sign. I know people find that hard to believe, but that's just the mystery of the ceremony. An eagle will hover right over you knowing that you're in ceremony. Thunder and lightning come by, and you just endure it. It's no problem. Lightning can be flashing all around you, and you'll laugh. The Great Spirit is not going to take your life up there while you are vision questing.[8]

Buddhist Four Subline States

Another way to a fuller realization of the spiritual side of the "Y" triangle can be found in meditating on the Buddhist four sublime states of mind known under the name *Brahma-vihara*. These four states are equanimity, compassion, loving-kindness, and sympathetic joy. They can form the foundation for a mind void of hatred as hatred is not compatible with these states. Benefits of deep meditation on them "will make these four qualities sink deep into the heart so that they become spontaneous attitudes not easily overthrown."[9]

Yoga

Yoga meditation is another way of greatly enriching both a person's physical and spiritual well-being. It is built upon centuries of tradition that aim to discover the unity of the self with the world and universe. Such meditation combines the ability to unify body and soul in seeking to find a richer fulfillment. In *A Beginners Guide to Meditation*, Maria Carico expresses yoga meditation as "an exquisite methodology [that] exists within the yoga tradition that is designed to reveal the interconnectedness of every living thing. This fundamental unity is referred to as *advaita*. Meditation is the actual experience of this union."[10]

Achieving a sense of personal harmony in the "Y" triangle is a lifelong quest. While this is unfolding, it is also important to consider one's core values relative to the core values of our democratic society.

PERSONAL MEDITATION ON AMERICA'S COMMON CORE VALUES

Common core values of our democracy are those that are generally recognized by the greater American society and are accepted because they are part of our nation's deepest philosophy. They are the soul of America. Important touchstones in the evolution of our nation's core values include the Declaration of Independence; the U.S. Constitution and Bill of Rights; the 13th, 14th, 15th, and 19th Amendments to the U.S. Constitution; *Brown v. Board of Education* Supreme Court Decision; the Civil Rights Act of 1964 and the Voting Rights Act of 1965.

These core values can be visualized in the following key touchstones of our evolving democratic history (figure 8.2).

Important common elements of these touchstones are the establishment of values such as:

- equality;
- equal protection of laws, due process;
- freedom of religion, speech, press, assembly.

Unfortunately high-stakes testing often eliminates social studies and the teaching/learning of these touchstones from a school's actual curriculum. Many teachers, especially at the elementary level, have been told that even though social studies is included in the published curriculum they should ignore it and teach math instead.[11] One Philadelphia fourth-grade teacher wrote on October 2021: "Social studies and science classes are only taught one or the other for a mere forty-five minutes once a day. . . . These nonessential subjects are being left out, and students can no longer enjoy them because of high-stakes testing."[12]

Figure 8.2 Soul of Our Nation. *Source*: Author Created.

Students are not the only ones with a lack of in-depth knowledge regarding our nation's touchstone values. Many educators at all levels have admitted to having only a superficial knowledge of these key core values.[13] Understanding their history and inherent importance is critical if our democracy is going to not only continue its existence but flourish as well. For these reasons, let us examine some ways to go more deeply into each one of them. Some consider the Declaration of Independence to be the most significant, so let us begin there.

Declaration of Independence

The U.S. Declaration of Independence (1776) is the first key touchstone of our democracy. Thomas Jefferson, and the committee with whom he wrote, summarized the philosophy of John Locke its own way when it wrote, "we hold these truths to be self-evident, that all men [and women][14] are created equal. They are endowed by their Creator with certain unalienable rights. That among these are life, liberty, and the pursuit of happiness."[15]

In meditating on this famous expression, individuals could begin by reading, if time permits, Carl Becker's *The Declaration of Independence: A Study on the History of Political Ideas*.[16] This would provide a rich context for a further deconstruction of the document. Individuals could also move directly to an examination of some keywords or expressions without reading Becker's account. They could deconstruct the phrases or words and ask what meaning they have for them and whether or not they are part of their core values.

For example "we" resonates with the idea of community rather than the individual "I." "Truths" indicates something that is authentic and cannot be discarded. "Self-evident" signifies a truth that is obvious, and "created equal" is at the heart of John Locke's revolutionary philosophy (and subsequently Jefferson's) that power resides in the people—all of the people.

The U.S. Constitution and Bill of Rights

The Constitution was written in 1787 at a convention in Philadelphia. It was ratified and became law in 1789. It replaced the ineffective Articles of Confederation and is based upon the principles laid out by John Locke in his *Second Treatise of Government*. In this treatise, Locke advocates for the power of the state to reside in the people rather than a supreme monarch or authority. This concept was radical at the time and it labeled Locke a revolutionary. His words inspired Thomas Jefferson and the committee who wrote the Declaration of Independence that led to our own revolution.

Another of Locke's major contributions to the Constitution was the concept of separation of powers. This separation was designed to prohibit the legislative, executive, and judicial functions of government from becoming centralized in one authority. The first of the three branches, the legislative, was divided further between the House of Representative and the Senate. The House was to be more representative of the people and therefore had an age requirement of twenty-five years and a two-year term office. This is compared with the Senate where the age requirement is thirty years of age and a six-year term of office.

The first ten amendments to the U.S. Constitution are known as the Bill of Rights. Written by James Madison, they were a response to Anti-Federalists' views that such an enumeration of rights was needed to protect individual liberties. The first of these is generally considered the foundation safeguarding citizens' rights. It states:

> Congress shall make no law respecting an establishment of religion, or prohibiting the free exercise thereof; or abridging the freedom of speech, or of the press; or the right of the people peaceably to assemble, and to petition the government for a redress of grievances.[17]

Deconstruction and meditation on these key rights would include an examination of an individual's tolerance for differing religious views, acceptance of diverse opinions of speech, and recognition of the important role of an independent press. Dialogue could also include placing these rights in the current cultural and political context and determining if they are viable or if they are in danger of extinction.

13th, 14th, 15th, and 19th Amendments to the Constitution

These four amendments can be considered our Human Rights Amendments. The 13th, 14th, and 15th are also known as the Civil War or Reconstruction Amendments. The 13th abolished slavery (1865), the 14th granted citizenship and established due process for former slaves (1868), and the 15th (1870) granted former slaves the right to vote. These amendments were passed by Reconstruction/Republican Congresses and ratified by similar Reconstruction state legislatures.[18]

Unfortunately, the Civil War Amendments became practically meaningless once federal troops were withdrawn from the South following the compromise of 1876 that ceded the disputed presidential election to the Republican Rutherford B. Hayes. Political, economic, and social power reverted to those who were in control during the Ante-Bellum period. This reversion raises once again the important question as to who won the Civil War (see chapter 2 for an elaboration of this concept).

Deconstruction of these amendments might include becoming more familiar with the Civil War and Reconstruction. One excellent documentary on these topics is Henry Louis Gates, Jr.'s *Reconstruction, America after the Civil War* which streams on Public Broadcasting System (PBS).[19] Another is MSNBC's documentary, *Civil War*.[20]

The 19th Amendment (1920) guaranteed women the right to vote and thereby doubled the number of citizens who could meaningfully participate in America's democracy. It simply states that "the right of citizens of the United States to vote shall not be denied or abridged by the United States or by any State on account of sex."[21] Beginning in the mid-1800s, thousands of suffragettes, led most prominently by Susan B. Anthony and Elizabeth Cady Stanton, braved demonstrations, marches, hunger strikes, insults, injuries, and countless hours of torment to see these words change our political world.

Background for deconstruction of this amendment might include viewing the powerful documentary that was produced by the National Endowment of the Humanities to mark the 2020 anniversary of the amendment's ratification. It is available for streaming at Public Broadcasting System (PBS), American Experience, *The Vote*.[22] An excellent book on the suffragettes is Lisa Tetrault's *The Myth of Seneca Falls*.

These background materials may provide a context to examine a person's beliefs, attitudes, and actions toward women's rights relative to equal opportunities for advancement in the workplace, equal pay, educational equity, and gender-based violence.

Brown v. Board of Education Supreme Court Decision

In 1951, third grader Linda Brown, a Black child, was denied admission to a segregated White school near her home in Topeka Kansas. Little did she or her father Oliver, who filed a lawsuit over the denial, realize at that time that their names would be associated with one of the most significant Supreme Court cases in our nation's history. In 1954, a unanimous Court ruled that segregated schools were inherently unequal. Chief Justice Earl Warren, who wrote the majority opinion, stated: "We conclude that in the field of public education the doctrine of 'separate but equal' has no place. Separate educational facilities are inherently unequal."[23]

These powerful words overturned the concept of separate but equal that an earlier Supreme Court had ruled was constitutional in *Plessy v. Ferguson* (1896). The 1954 decision breathed new life into the 14th Amendment's equal protection clause and was a monumental step toward ending legalized segregation of our nation's schools.

Ending the legal aspects of segregation did not by itself integrate public schools.

Desegregation efforts throughout the nation, but especially in the South, were often accompanied by ugly violence. Perhaps the most notorious example was the admission of Black students to the all-White Central high school in Little Rock Arkansas in 1957.

Known as the "Little Rock Nine," Black students bravely marched through angry mobs who were spitting and yelling all types of racial slurs at them. Upon reaching the school they realized they were barred from entry. Governor Orval Faubus had ordered the Arkansas National Guard to permit Whites safe passage but to deny the same for Blacks. It was not until President Dwight Eisenhower sent the army's 101st Airborne Division and federalized the Arkansas Nation Guard that the Black students were admitted to the school.

Desegregation has been a difficult process and has involved schools in all regions of the country. Boston, Cleveland, Chicago, and Detroit are just four examples of major cities that were ordered by Federal courts to desegregate their schools. These orders were met with resistance and violence similar to that which occurred throughout the South. De facto segregation—segregation not sanctioned by law but by practice—continues to create substantial challenges for school integration in most urban/suburban areas.

There are many video documentaries and books that provide a rich and often dramatic context for a deeper understanding of the seismic effects of the *Brown* decision. Some of the documentaries are *Eyes on the Prize: America's Civil Rights Movement, The Road to Brown, Little Rock Central: 50 Years Later*, and *Hoxie: The First Stand*.

Kaitlin Smith presents a description of each of these and others in "6 Resources That Look at the History and Legacy of Brown v. Board of Education." Ways to stream these can be found at https://facingtoday.facinghistory.org/6-resources-that-look-at-the-history-and-legacy-of-brown-v-board-of-education.

Civil Rights Act 1964, Voting Rights Act 1965

Both the Civil Rights Act of 1964 and the Voting Rights Act of 1965 are considered landmark acts of Congress. They were passed in attempts to rectify the failure of the Reconstruction Amendments (13th, 14th, and 15th) to grant basic rights of citizenship to former slaves and their descendants. The Civil Rights Act (July 2, 1964) prohibits discrimination on the basis of race, color, religion, sex, or national origin. Sexual orientation and gender identity were added on June 15, 2020, when the Supreme Court ruled that they were lawful categories under Title VII of the 1964 act.

The effects of the Civil Rights Act have been enormous. It provides Blacks equal access to public facilities such as restaurants and transportation. Such access had been barred throughout the post Reconstruction South by Jim Crow laws designed to keep the races segregated. An award-winning 2018 movie, *Green Book*, is an engaging look at the effects of racial segregation that the Civil Rights Act of 1964 was designed to prohibit.

The Voting Rights Act of 1965 was specifically aimed at post Reconstruction laws, such as literacy tests, that repressed Black voters in the South. Civil rights leaders planned a major protest against these restrictions by marching from Selma, Alabama, to the state capital Montgomery. On March 7, 1965, approximately 600 peaceful marchers were stopped at the Edmund Pettus Bridge by Alabama state troopers and sheriff deputies. Marchers were tear-gassed and brutally beaten with clubs and whips. Fifty-eight protestors were injured including John Lewis, head of the Student Nonviolent Coordinating Committee, whose skull was fractured.

The encounter is remembered as "Bloody Sunday," and Lewis testified at a Congressional hearing that began the week following the event. An account of John Lewis's testimony including copies of his exact words is available at the following site: https://www.archives.gov/exhibits/eyewitness/html.php?section=2. On March 17, at the end of the hearing, Judge Frank Johnson, Jr., ruled that the protestors had a right to march. This opened the door for more than 3,200 demonstrators, under the protection of federal troops, to march from Selma to Montgomery on Mach 21, 1965.

"Bloody Sunday" was widely publicized, and the brutality stunned the nation's conscience. Under President Lyndon Johnson's leadership, the Voting Rights Act was passed by Congress five months later on August 6, 1965. John Lewis continued to be active in civil rights issues and was eventually elected to the U.S. House of Representatives from Georgia's fifth district in 1986.

John Lewis remained passionate about civil rights issues until his death on July 17, 2020. He returned to the Edmund Pettus Bridge regularly to commemorate "Bloody Sunday." The last time was on July 26, 2020, when two black/brown horses pulled a wagon upon which his coffin rested on the bridge across the Alabama River. Rose petals were strewn on the roadway—a far cry from the clubs and racial slurs that greeted him on March 7, 1965.

SUMMARY: LESSONS LEARNED

- Leadership, especially transformational leadership, springs from within.
- Four pillars of success that enabled the Jesuits to survive for more than 460 years are self-awareness, ingenuity, love, and heroism.
- The "Y" tagline of mind, spirit, body is a reminder that personal meditation needs to be included with daily physical exercise and intellectual activity.
- Regular meditation on America's common core values is necessary to be a transformational leader within our democracy.

- Five touchstones are keys to being an effective transformational leader who is knowledgeable regarding America's common core values. These touchstones are the Declaration of Independence; the U.S. Constitution and Bill of Rights; the 13th, 14th, 15th, and 19th Amendments to the U.S. Constitution; *Brown v. Board of Education* Supreme Court Decision; and the Civil Rights Act of 1964 and the Voting Rights Act of 1965.

The next chapter, "Creating Communities of Learners," presents practical examples of some ways that transformational leaders can create professional learning communities among teachers and other educational leaders. It also presents ways of engaging the public through various forms of public pedagogy.

NOTES

1. Chris Lowney, *Heroic Leadership* (Chicago: Loyola Press, 2003), 15.
2. Ibid., 20.
3. The number of men considered Jesuits in 2021 is approximately 16,000. This includes priests, novices, scholastics, and brothers. For a full description of the Jesuits see https://www.jesuits.org/about-us/the-jesuits/.
4. Lowney, *Heroic Leadership*, 9.
5. John I: 37–39, *Good News New Testament* (New York: American Bible Society, 1976).
6. Roger Joslin, *Running the Spiritual Path* (New York: St. Martin's Griffin, 2003), 230.
7. Ibid., 231.
8. Ed McGaa Eagle Man, "Eagle man's vision quest," http://native-americans-online.com/native-american-vision-quest.html (accessed December 5, 2017).
9. Nyanaponika Thera, "The four sublime states, contemplations on love, compassion, sympathetic joy, and equanimity."
10. Maria Carico, *A Beginners Guide to Meditation*, https://www.yogajournal.com/meditation/let-s-meditate (accessed December 5, 2017).
11. This author first became aware of this in 2004 when a fifth-grade teacher in Philadelphia gave him an email from the building principal that told teachers not to teach social students from October until April. This allotted time was to be used to concentrate on math instead because the benchmark standardized tests showed a math deficiency. In recent conversations with several educators, this practice appears not to be an anomaly as late as October, 2021.
12. Richard Levy, "To test or not to test," Unpublished paper for a class at Saint Joseph's University, October 21, 2021.
13. This author briefly surveyed twelve doctoral students in a Law and Policy course in the summer of 2021 regarding their knowledge of these key touchstones.

Overall, the results were that most had only a limited knowledge of their history or value.

14. Author added.

15. The United States Declaration of Independence, https://www.archives.gov/founding-docs/declaration-transcript (accessed December 5, 2017).

16. Carl Becker, *The Declaration of Independence: A Study on the History of Political Ideas* (New York: Harcourt, Brace and Co.), 1922.

17. Bill of Rights of the United States of America (1791), http://www.billofrightsinstitute.org/founding-documents/bill-of-rights/ (accessed December 11, 2017).

18. The Republican Party during this time was the party of Lincoln that advocated a far-reaching social, political, and economic reconstruction of the postwar South. The Democratic Party became the party of those who favored the Confederacy and separation from the Union. The two parties have substantially reversed positions beginning with the civil rights activism of the 1960s.

19. Henry Louis Gates Jr., *Reconstruction, America after the Civil War*, Public Broadcasting System, https://www.pbs.org/weta/reconstruction/ (accessed October 24, 2021).

20. Brad Pitt and Henry Louis Gates, Jr., *Civil War*, MSNBC, https://www.msnbc.com/msnbc/watch/civil-war-official-trailer-a-feature-documentary-123102277716 (accessed October 24, 2021).

21. Nineteenth Amendment, United States Constitution (1920), https://constitution.congress.gov/constitution/amendment-19/ (accessed October 2, 2021).

22. Public Broadcasting System (PBS), American Experience "The Vote," https://www.google.com/search?q=PBS+documentary+The+Vote&oq=PBS+documentary+The+Vote&aqs=chrome.69i57j0i22i30.6024j0j15&sourceid=chrome&ie=UTF-8 (accessed October 24, 2021).

23. Earl Warren, Majority opinion in *Brown v. Board of Education*, 1954, https://americanhistory.si.edu/brown/history/5-decision/courts-decision.html (accessed October 25, 2021).

Chapter 9

Creating Communities of Learners

Community cannot be produced simply through rational formulation nor through edict. Like freedom, it has to be achieved by persons offered the space in which to discover what they recognize together and appreciate in common . . . it ought to be a space infused by the kind of imaginative awareness that enables those involved to imagine alternative possibilities for their own becoming and their group's becoming.[1]

—Maxine Greene

Maxine Greene (1917–2014) was a distinguished professor in the foundations of education at Teachers College, Columbia University, from 1975 to 1998. She was a strong promoter of the progressive theories and social justice ideals of the highly influential progressive educator, John Dewey. Greene believed that school leaders need to provide space and time for the formation of communities of learners that use aesthetic education to release individuals' imaginations. In this way, new connections and innovations can "imagine alternative possibilities for their own becoming and their group's becoming."

PROFESSIONAL LEARNING COMMUNITIES

Professional development for educators often consists of one-shot sessions that impart information and, occasionally, inspiration. Oftentimes such information and inspiration last only as long as the sessions themselves. These are often shallow and do little to build vital communities that honor educators as professionals. They seldom include intellectual and emotional experiences that reach deeply into participants' minds and souls. Hardly ever do they involve aesthetics or engage with challenging professional literature. Rarely do they consider, in meaningful ways, the core values that are touchstones of America's soul.

This chapter will explore ways to create professional learning communities through sustained professional development. Such development can challenge participants intellectually and emotionally as they:

- share aesthetic experiences;
- engage with challenging professional literature;
- engage with award-winning literature;
- consider the touchstones that form our core values as a nation and society.

Creating Professional Learning Communities through Shared Aesthetic Experiences

Opening teacher meetings that begin a school year usually follow a formula that begins with a meeting of the school district's entire faculty at a central location. It is at this meeting that central office leaders, usually led by the school superintendent, present challenges that threaten public education and goals for the year. These sessions, lasting approximately one and one-half to two hours, usually end with an attempt at an inspirational message asking the teachers to do their best during difficult times.

The next part of the day usually focuses on the introduction of some new initiatives or specific departmental meetings. These are followed by lunch before teachers report to their building meetings where the real action begins. It is here that the principal imparts specific building information (fire drill and lockdown procedures, bussing and/or walker schedules, lunchtimes, discipline procedures, etc.). Finally, similar to the central office meeting, the principal attempts an inspirational message that, again, asks teachers to do their best during challenging times.

This formula, especially at the building level, is often successful in building some surface communities. After two and one-half months of summer leave—time spent on university campuses, part-time jobs, and vacations—colleagues renew acquaintances and friendships. Academic departments and grade-level partners begin to plan the all-important specifics related to the arrival of the students.

While this formula and the renewal of surface communities are a way to begin a school year, Maxie Greene inspires us to dig deeper and try to create communities where untapped energy abounds with educational possibilities yet unimagined. Greene's inspiration challenged leaders in the Owen J. Roberts school district to try something very different one year for the faculty's opening day.

Recognizing that Philadelphia has an amazing number of cultural institutions, the district's leaders planned a full opening-day field trip to explore some of them. Approximately 200 teachers and school leaders began with a morning visit to the Academy of Music, then the home of the Philadelphia Orchestra. Although the Orchestra was not in session, teachers sat on the stage and listened to Orchestra personnel describe various programs that were available for students and faculty.

Next was lunch at the Franklin Institute and time to explore some of the world-famous exhibits and participate in numerous hands-on activities. This was followed by an afternoon at the Philadelphia Museum of Art. Museum personnel organized the teachers into ten different groups—each with a different theme. Art docents then led tours through the museum following each of the distinctive themes. The universal experience of being together in the museum was in this way deepened with a richness available only through more intimate groupings. Following the tours, participants were heard sharing with colleagues what they learned on their specific tour.

Nearly 100 percent of the faculty participated in the field trip. While no pre- or posttests were given, the overwhelming feedback of the experience was a big thumbs-up. Many indicated that they had either not been to these cultural resources previously or had not visited them in many years.

An interesting side note was the reaction of the football coaches. They did not want to spend an entire day on the trip. There was an opening game within a few days, and they wanted extra time to prepare for it. The building principal told them that their attendance was not optional. When the trip was over, they were among the most vocal in praise of the field trip. This was echoed by faculty members from across grade levels. They were generally upbeat as they rode buses together, broke bread with each other, and shared new experiences.

It is difficult to know whether there was much carryover of this experience into various aspects of school curricula and activities. One activity, however, showed at least one positive effect. This occurred near the end of the fall semester when a high school art teacher collaborated with a music teacher to provide some students with an unusual interdisciplinary experience. Each teacher selected fifteen students and arranged for a visit to a rehearsal of the Philadelphia Orchestra. Rehearsals of the highly professional ensemble are nearly the same as attending an evening concert. One big difference—rehearsals are free.

The bus ride to the Academy of Music was itself interesting as students interacted with others whom they may have met for the first time. Most had never been to the ornate Academy of Music, and, upon entrance, their comments reflected that they were taken aback. The assignment for the art students was to sketch whatever they wanted. They would later make acrylic paintings of their sketches which would be shared with the music students. Many of the paintings were of the hall itself while others were of musicians performing on various instruments.

Many of the music students stated that this was the first time they had been to a live classical concert. One student, in particular, a high school junior named Benjamin Britten (no relation to the famous British composer of the same name), said that this was his first classical concert. He had been thinking about making music part of his college plans. This concert so inspired him that it confirmed his desire, and he planned to make that thought a reality.

It is unimportant to know if this ever happened. What is important is that for this particular student, on this particular day, a powerful aesthetic experience touched his soul. In this account, Maxine Greene's words came alive when she wrote that aesthetic experiences should contain "a space infused by the kind of imaginative awareness that enables those involved to imagine alternative possibilities for their own becoming."[2]

The day following this Philadelphia Orchestra field trip, a meeting of twelve school superintendents was held in Harrisburg with the Secretary of Education, Charles Zogby. Zogby was a new appointee and was reaching out to superintendents to gain their support for high-stakes state testing. He advocated for an emphasis to be placed on reading, language arts, and math. Other subjects, including the arts, could be reduced or eliminated altogether. The Owen J. Roberts superintendent shared Benjamin Britten's story. Zogby's reaction? Silence.

School administrators can become transformational educational leaders through various activities—common field trips, sharing meals together, playing team sports, social gatherings, and others. One of the most powerful is by bonding through the common reading of thought-provoking books that further the growth of participants and help shape the mission of the school.

Creating Professional Learning Communities by Bonding through Books

Most of us can probably remember times when in certain classes—elementary through graduate school—the subject matter was rich, and through substantive dialogue, students actually became classmates and colleagues. Professional learning communities of teachers and other school personnel can be created in a similar way. The inherent energy within these communities can then help tackle various issues, turn dull schools into exciting places of learning, and create the future rather than simply react to the present.

For example, in gaining a deeper understanding of the importance of a school's real mission versus the words in the mission statement, teachers might read H.G. Bissinger's *Friday Night Lights*.[3] The emphasis on Permian Panthers football and the feverish energy that builds toward winning a state championship is not found anywhere in the school's mission statement. Nonetheless, it is the energy—the "mojo"—at the Friday night games that unites a community and often is the most important driver of school activities. Dialogue on this inconsistency can be a springboard to a critical evaluation of participants' own school's mission and mission statement.

Another book that might be used to develop a school's mission would be John Dewey's *School and Society, Child and Curriculum*.[4] It is here that Dewey strongly advocates for the student to be at the center of both the school's curriculum and learning activities. Experiential learning will be long-lasting, as compared with the short-term learning associated with unrelated activities often imposed from outside of the classroom.

Considered a classic for understanding the growth of the efficiency movement in education is Raymond Callahan's *Education and the Cult of Efficiency*.[5] Callahan describes the powerful influence that Frederick W. Taylor's efficiency experts and time-study managers had in shaping the physical and academic aspects of today's schools. Callahan's description of "Schmidt's" transformation from a regular pig iron worker to a model of efficiency at Bethlehem Steel is both fascinating and frightening. Reading selected chapters—perhaps two, four, and five—will provide rich material for dialogue on the efficiency movement which led to today's emphasis on high-stakes testing.

A thought-provoking book that examines the history, influence, and effects of intelligence quotient (IQ) testing is Stephen Jay Gould's *The Mismeasure of Man*.[6] Gould traces ways that the original purpose of IQ tests was distorted by mass testing that grew rapidly during World War I. These tests were seen as an efficient way to sift and sort new military recruits to fit particular needs. His chapter entitled "The Hereditarian Theory of IQ: *An American Invention*" is particularly powerful and raises questions as to how and why we use these tests to sift and sort students into particular educational programs and tracts.

An insightful book for those seeking alternatives to high-stakes testing would be Grant Wiggins's *Assessing Student Performance*.[7] Wiggins presents persuasive arguments for authentic assessments that grow from a school's specific curriculum and teaching/learning activities. Such assessments should be individualized for each particular school and not standardized from some outside source. Selected chapters—such as one, two, seven, and eight—provide excellent alternatives to mandated state tests. The entire issue of testing and its effects on students and teachers usually leads to in-depth dialogue and a greater understanding of a school's real mission.

In a school or district that is trying to build a greater awareness of racial and social justice issues, broader forms of literature can often be very effective. Award-winning novels can offer unique perspectives and provide profound intellectual and emotional contexts to better understand complex social issues. They can be rich sources for individual and group introspection.

Creating Professional Learning Communities by Bonding through Award-Winning Literature

There are many award-winning pieces of literature that could be used to build professional learning communities while exploring issues of race and social justice. Two will be presented as they have proven to be particularly effective in leading to substantive dialogue. The first of these is Nobel Prize–winning author Toni Morrison's *The Bluest Eye*.[8]

Professional Development Using The Bluest Eye

Toni Morrison's first novel, *The Bluest Eye*, is extremely powerful in depicting the dominance that one culture can have not only over another but also over individuals within the dominated culture. Her main character, Pecola, truly is one of the saddest, most despairing characters in all of American literature. She wants blue eyes so that she can be similar to Disney's Cinderella or her idol, Shirley Temple. This Black girl can have neither.

Not being particularly attractive Pecola is the butt of merciless taunts. Her miserable home life eventually leads to her being raped and impregnated by her father. Her friends plant marigold seeds believing that they will flower and her baby will live. There were no marigolds that year—and no baby. Pecola becomes disconnected from everything around her and convinces herself that at least she finally has one thing—blue eyes.

Deep and sensitive dialogue regarding the far-reaching and deep-seated effects that cultural dominance can have in creating racial separation and hatred can be gained from several professional development sessions centered on this novel. It could be introduced to the group by viewing the beginning of the movie *The Littlest Rebel* (portions available on YouTube). Set in pre–Civil War years, the film stars Shirley Temple and Bill "Bojangles" Robinson.

The opening segment features Bojangles dancing at Virgie's (Shirley Temple) birthday party. After the dance, her mother calls her away for a brief meeting with some Black plantation children. When the Black children stumble over the reading of birthday greetings to her, Virgie becomes very condescending while appearing to be overly sweet. Today these segments are usually seen as a shocking depiction of poor race relations. At the time it was not. *The Littlest Rebel* was one of the top box-office draws of 1935.

Dialogue on the film can go in many directions. Some of these are the portrayal of slaves as being of inferior intelligence, failure to reconcile the effects of slavery to this day, and the supposed equality (and possibly equity) of all U.S. citizens as promised in our founding documents. The dialogue could also explore the acceptance or rejection of various historical depictions of race relations.

Creating Communities of Learners 145

This first dialogue session featuring *The Littlest Rebel* can lead to preparation for the next session with copies of *The Bluest Eye* given to all participants. This second session should be planned so that there is sufficient time to read the novel and prepare an activity to share with the group. One activity that has proven effective is to draw a design (or prepare a PowerPoint) that captures the essence of the novel. An example of a PowerPoint design prepared by the author is found in figure 9.1.

The blue eye in the center with a teardrop is an obvious reference to the book's title and the wretchedness of Pecola's life. The white picket fence behind it symbolizes Morrison's introduction of the novel with a presentation of Scott Foresman's Dick and Jane reading series and its depiction of the perfect White family. Perhaps some of you remember—Dick, Jane, Mother, Father, Sally, Spot, and Puff. The dead marigolds surrounding the eye and fence are the sad reminder of Pecola's anguish over her dead baby and her belief that she has at least gotten her blue eyes. The eye and fence are at the center of a cross—perhaps Pecola's crucifixion?

Sharing different designs at the next dialogue session will open the group to deep conversations that should eventually lead to a consideration of race relations in the school or the district. The group may decide to post several designs in the media center or some other place in the school.

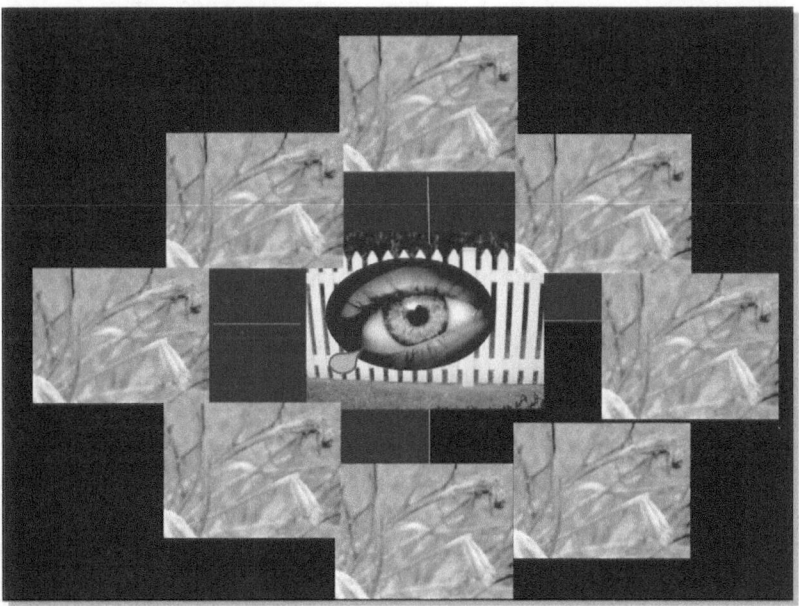

Figure 9.1 The Bluest Eye. *Source*: Author Created.

Another powerful novel for dialogue sessions is Tommy Orange's *There, There*.[9] This novel is based upon the distressed lives of Native Americans from different tribes whose hopes and dreams were often shattered after relocating to Oakland, California.

Professional Development Using There, There

Tommy Orange's first novel has been greeted with praise by critics as well as the public. It was chosen as a Philadelphia's "One Book, One Read" for 2020 and centers on the lives of twelve urbanized Native Americans who are going to participate in the Big Oakland Powwow. These stories capture the realities of life for many Native Americans following the federal government's encouragement and assistance to resettle them in urban areas.

These relocations, which began in the 1950s, often resulted in deeply stressful lives—a condition that continues to this day. According to a National Archives resource for educators entitled "American Indian Urban Relocation," "[Native Americans] struggled to adjust to life in a metropolis and faced unemployment, low-end jobs, discrimination, homesickness and the loss [of] traditional cultural supports."[10] Urban relocation was another attempt to bury the cultural identities of Native Americans—often known by the euphemism "assimilation"—someplace deep within the dominant European White culture.

In many respects, the urbanization policies were softer than the boarding school movement of the late 1800s and early 1900s. This movement attempted the reeducation and assimilation of Native American children. It resulted in the relocation of children from reservations to schools such as the Carlisle Indian Industrial School.

Here, among other culture-shattering regulations, children had their hair cut, were forced to wear military uniforms, drilled in formations, and memorized passages from the Bible. Their proud names, which connected them to their families and tribes, were changed to English ones such as Fanny, Mabel, or Curtis. Speaking their native languages often meant having their mouths washed out with lye.

The policies of urbanization were not as outwardly oppressive as the boarding schools. Nonetheless, the mental, social, emotional, and physical disconnects from cultural roots were inwardly wrenching. Tommy Orange, subtly and at the same time dramatically, captures these tensions in his narration of the despair, tedium, and drama involved with day-to-day survival.

Educators seeking deeper awareness of racial and social justice issues could begin by reading *There, There*. They could then attend dialogue sessions with their colleagues to begin uncovering the richness of the novel. An initial session might involve viewing a video of a book forum that was sponsored by the Politics and Prose at the Wharf bookstore which was held on July 25, 2018, in Washington D.C. A video of the forum is available on YouTube at https://www.youtube.com/watch?v=hsHNaoJbMlg.

At this forum, Orange read selections from two parts of his novel—the Prologue and a chapter entitled "Thomas Frank." This chapter was renamed "The State" and appeared as a separate story in March 26, 2018, *New Yorker*. Orange's reading of these two selections inspires us to elevate our eyes to look deeply into the soul of America and see both a painful history and an uncertain vision of the future.

One example of this elevation is the description he presents regarding the verbal transmission of Native American cultures from one generation to another. The book's Prologue describes several brutal massacres and dehumanizing atrocities committed by Whites on Native Americans. Orange states that the pain associated with these horrific events often prevents elders from sharing the past. Instead of cultural transmission, there is erasure.

Another example of soul-searching is his chapter entitled "Jacquie Red Feather." Her struggle with alcoholism and attempts to find some semblance of happiness is deeply moving. In addressing both alcoholism and high suicides rates among Native Americans, Orange compares many of their desperate living conditions with individuals trapped in a burning building. Some would rather jump than remain inside and be burned alive.

Other chapters of *There, There* are just as powerful as "Jacquie Red Feather." Groups or individuals could read different ones and report back to the entire community at subsequent dialogue sessions. Another activity might be the preparation of questions to ask Tommy Orange if he were there in person. It might even be possible to connect with him via the internet or actually have him come to a special session.

Many other pieces of literature—including Amanda Gorman's 2021 Inaugural Poem—could be used for additional dialogue sessions. Generally, when powerful literature is used for substantive sessions two remarkable transformations happen. The person leading the dialogue, rather than administering someone else's ideas or mandates, becomes the intellectual and effective leader of the group. The second is that many other leaders emerge as the group changes from being a "group" and becomes a community of learners.

Another important way to build professional learning communities is by bonding through a greater understanding of America's core values. Such understandings are the lifeblood that sustain our democracy. Knowledge of them is the responsibility of all educators. A particular burden falls upon leaders who have the power to make this happen through sustained professional development.

Creating Professional Learning Communities by Bonding through America's Core Values

Many teachers, from preschool through high school, have only a surface understanding of America's core values. In the previous chapter ("Becoming Transformational Educational Leaders through Personal Growth"), these are described as touchstones and include the Declaration of Independence; the United States Constitution and Bill of Rights; the 13th, 14th, 15th, and 19th Amendments to the United States Constitution; *Brown v. Board of Education* Supreme Court Decision; the Civil Rights Act of 1964; and the Voting Rights Act of 1965.

Important common elements of these touchstones are the establishment of values such as:

- equality;
- equal protection of laws, due process;
- freedom of religion, speech, press, and assembly.

Teachers, as well as the students they see daily, possess these basic rights. As indicated in the previous chapter, one of the unfortunate effects of high-stakes testing is the cutback or virtual elimination of social studies from our school curricula. Many teachers, especially at the elementary level, have been told that even though social studies is included in the published curriculum they should ignore it and teach math instead.[11]

One of the best guarantees that the values contained in each of these touchstones remains a vital part of America's soul is to understand them in some detail. Valuable dialogue sessions for teachers regarding each of them can be designed by the school's educational leaders working with their history and social studies teachers. A guide to facilitating sessions could be similar to that which is presented in chapter 8 where the introspection and growth of individual leaders regarding the touchstones is presented.

The success of professional learning communities prepares educators to become leaders and move to the next important phase in creating "Communities of Learners." This involves expanding the "school" to include the greater community and engage the public through various means of public pedagogy.

This is a natural step as schools and school districts are usually of central importance in their particular geographic communities. They are often the largest employer, run the biggest bus fleet, serve the most meals on a yearly basis, own the largest real estate holdings, collect the most taxes, and purchase a multitude of services that return money to the community. The challenge for education leaders is to turn geographic communities into dynamic communities of learners wherein the core values of the school district are formed and reinforced. This can be done through public pedagogy.

TRANSFORMATIONAL EDUCATIONAL LEADERSHIP AND PUBLIC PEDAGOGY

Transformational educational leaders are those who look for opportunities to engage the public in dialogue regarding their schools. They recognize the importance they have in shaping the future not for only individual students but entire school districts. Such leaders do not accept the role of schools in a democracy as being that of merely transmitting the past but see it as a driving force to create the future. In 2021, opportunities for transformational leadership greatly increased with the rise of challenges associated with Critical Race Theory (CRT).

CRT and Chaos

Beginning in the summer of 2021 opportunities for transformational educational leaders to engage in public pedagogy expanded exponentially. Considerations over ways that the dynamics of race relations as well as the history of racism should be taught in our schools coalesced around three words—Critical Race Theory. Battles in the streets moved to hostile encounters at school board meetings. School board members, superintendents, and other educators were faced with intense, often hostile, public outcries not seen in decades. Citizens lined up at school board meetings to express their views as to ways that issues of race should be addressed in schools. Let us consider one example that happened in June 2021.

On June 14, 2021, an unusual event took place at the Tredyffrin-Easttown school board meeting. This school district, located on the affluent Mainline outside of Philadelphia, is generally rated as one of the top five districts in Pennsylvania. It is known for its forward-thinking leadership and enlightened approach to providing high-quality education for its 7,200 students.

What was unusual on June 14 was the public comment section of the board meeting. For more than two and one-half hours, thirty-three individuals spoke passionately about their experiences regarding the presence or absence of systemic racism in the school district. They also addressed the district's initiatives regarding racial equity and their perceived concerns over CRT. Many comments focused on CRT as residents had been encouraged to attend the meeting by social media messages posted by "Parents fighting Critical Race Theory in the T/E school district."[12]

Tredyffrin-Easttown was not the only school district to experience issues related to CRT Angry demonstrations at school board meetings swept across the country. *The Washington Post* on June 23 reported that a contentious meeting held the previous evening in Loudoun County, Virginia, was dominated by two issues—transgender rights and CRT. The newspaper stated: "The tense gathering was marked by outbursts, insults and recriminations before a unanimous vote by the school board halted the proceedings and police cleared the hall."[13]

Reactions to CRT Chaos: Authentic Dialogue and Strategic Planning

School leaders' reactions to the chaos surrounding CRT varied in the two examples presented above. In Tredyffrin-Easttown, board members and administrators listened stoically until all citizens had spoken. At the end of the public comment section, some board members did offer their personal perspectives but did not enter into dialogue with the public. Loudoun County also had a public comment at its board meeting. In this case, however, the anger of the speakers boiled over, and the school board "halted the proceedings and police cleared the hall."[14]

School board meetings are structured to conduct the business of the district. They are not designed to encourage dialogue with the public. This arrangement does very little to build a community of learners and often perpetuates division and hostility. Transformational leaders need to create other spaces for authentic dialogue, especially when considering controversial issues such as CRT Such dialogue should be based upon true listening and open sharing of accurate information and differing perspectives.

A good description of authentic dialogue is found in the writing of Alexander Sidorkin. His writing was previously described in chapter 3. It is important, and therefore, worth repeating here.

Sidorkin's concept of dialogue is far more attuned with human rather than organizational qualities. He wrote that "We are human in the fullest sense when we engage in dialogue."[15] He contends further that dialogue is not a process or means to accomplish some other aim. It by itself is the goal. He stated this concept as follows: "Dialogue is an end in itself, the very essence of human existence."[16]

This conception of dialogue requires a democratic context in which all beings are viewed with inherent equality and dignity. Within such a context, it is possible to relate fully with another human being. When this relationship occurs, important dialogue happens. This relationship, in Sidorkin's words, "takes you completely out of your regular life."[17]

To encourage this type of dialogue, transformational leaders need to schedule sessions at different times, and possibly in different places. These sessions should be separated from regular school board meetings. One example could be rotating sessions at varied times to different neighborhood schools. The agenda for these sessions could be open or could focus on particular controversial issues such as CRT.

Another invaluable tool to help achieve authentic dialogue is the strategic-planning process that most districts conduct on a regular basis. Some states, such as Pennsylvania, have a specific format that districts follow in developing their plans. In other cases, a number of strategic-planning models are available. One valuable resource is William Cook's *Strategic Planning for American's Schools*.[18]

Strategic plans can be thought of as an essential blueprint—or a compass—to set the district's priorities and guide its actions for a specified period of time. At the end of that time, the plan is evaluated as to its effectiveness. An outline of Cook's strategic-planning process is presented below in sequential order:

- beliefs,
- mission,
- policies,
- internal analysis,
- external Analysis,
- objectives,
- strategies,
- action plans.

While each of these components is important in developing a good plan, the most critical are the first two—beliefs and mission. In creating a mission statement that reflects the core beliefs of the district's citizens is where dialogue can happen most productively. It is here that public pedagogy at the highest level can occur. An example of this is presented when the Owen J. Roberts School District set out to "build a lighthouse" during a time when the district was in the midst of a crisis not unlike that associated with CRT.

Developing a District Mission Statement: "Let's Build a Lighthouse"

The first step in effective strategic planning is for educational leaders to facilitate the development of a mission statement that truly belongs to the community. Once developed, this statement should be the critical standard for policy development, curriculum design, personnel procedures, financial decisions, and other district activities.

The Owen J. Roberts school district was mired in a brutal controversy over school prayer (see chapter 3—"The Power of Symbols: Auschwitz,

Anti-Semitism and a School Prayer Crisis"). In the midst of this crisis, district leaders and the school board began a strategic-planning process to help determine the core beliefs of the community. The process began with the development of a mission statement and was called "Mission 21." It was planned to be a propelling force to take the district well into the twenty-first century.

At one of the initial dialogue session designed to develop a mission statement, one of the citizens suggested using a symbol of a lighthouse to create a visual that would embody the essence of the district's mission. This lighthouse would be used to guide the actions of the district. The lighthouse base and beacons were created by input from the district's students, parents, teachers, support staff members, and citizens. This input began with a widely distributed questionnaire that asked four basic questions:

- What purpose do you think education has in our democratic society?
- What do you think is the most important skill for students to have by the time they graduate from high school?
- What do you think is the most important value or attitude for students to have by the time they graduate from high school?
- If you could improve one thing about the curriculum of the school district, what would that be?

More than 650 students, recent graduates, staff members, and community residents responded to the survey. These responses were reviewed, categorized, and used to write a mission statement that reflected this input. The statement recognized the importance of developing both cognitive learning (skills and knowledge acquisition) as well as attitudes (values and human relations concepts).

The mission statement was synthesized into a graphic representation of a lighthouse. The foundation consisted of educational processes important across all skill areas: problem-solving, analytical and creative thinking, and study skills. The main body of the lighthouse included the curricular areas of communications, math, social studies, science, fine arts, physical education, health, and various vocational areas. The lighthouse beacons represented the important values in the statement: positive self-esteem, personal responsibility, honesty and integrity, social and environmental responsibility, respect and concern for others, and positive attitudes.[19]

The lighthouse image was sent to Owen J. Roberts's staff and community. It was well received and guided district actions for several years (figure 9.2).

Focusing on education and designing a mission statement in this manner built an important bridge in Owen J. Roberts across the school prayer divide. A similar process, away from heated rhetoric and hostile outbursts, could be used to open dialogue regarding the definition and history of CRT. It could

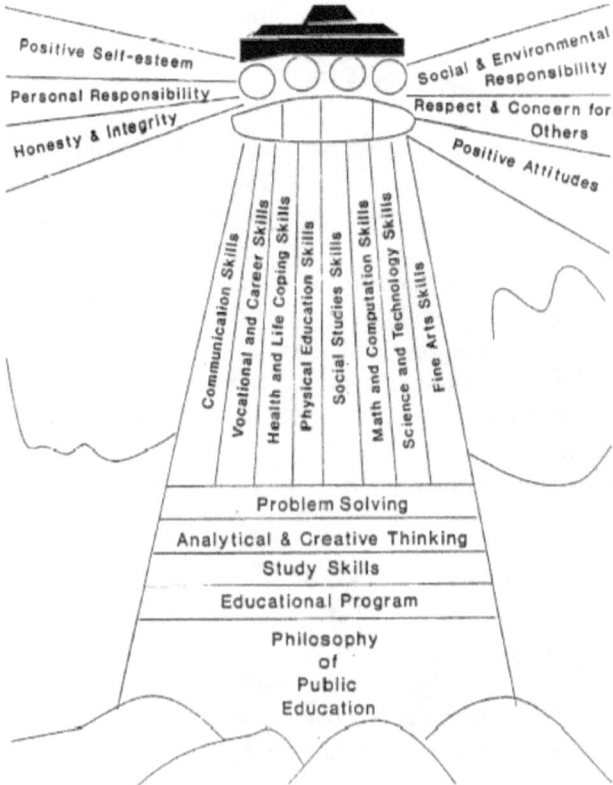

Figure 9.2 Representation of the Lighthouse. *Source:* Author Created.

also provide forums to develop further the district's goals regarding the teaching of racism and racial history.

Communicating the Mission Statement

In addition to leading in the development of the district's mission statement, transformational educational leaders are also responsible for communicating it to various constituencies in the district. Active engagement with the public should go beyond publishing the statement on the district's website. Leaders need to be masters of communication strategies. Building communications bridges into the community is a way to learn the views and values of a variety of citizens. It also opens doors for conversations on various school issues such as the district's mission.

Here are some practical strategies for building communication bridges. Transformational educational leaders could:

- become active in at least one service organization (examples may include Lions, Kiwanis, and Rotary clubs);
- approach local newspapers and offer to write a weekly or monthly guest column;
- approach local radio and T.V. stations and offer to host a regular call-in talk show that features various aspects of the school district;
- contact area realtors and prepare various presentations or open houses in the schools;
- prepare and distribute an annual paper calendar to all residents (not just school parents) that provides both practical information (school times, transportation information, lunch arrangements, weather cancellations, virtual learning, school board meetings) and the mission, statements of purpose, synopsis of district budget, student achievements, and demographics of the district;
- develop special programs for senior citizens that may include pairing them with students as well as sponsoring special events such as a "senior prom";
- become knowledgeable of and reach out to special interest organizations such as the N.A.A.C.P;
- join the local chamber of commerce;
- sponsor a "community appreciation night" as an occasion when board members can bring guests at no cost to a sporting event;
- reach out to local churches who may have joint meetings over breakfast or some other collaborative event;
- lead the schools in participation in events such as Relay for Life;
- _____ (add your own unique strategies).

Utilization of these strategies enable transformational educational leaders to build a foundation to unify the school district through the identification and development of common interests, goals, values, and a sense of mission. This is the essence of a "community of learners" and an example of public pedagogy at the highest level.

We began this chapter with a quotation of Maxine Greene. It seems fitting to end this chapter, as well as this book, with the same quotation:

> Community cannot be produced simply through rational formulation nor through edict. Like freedom, it has to be achieved by persons offered the space in which to discover what they recognize together and appreciate in common . . . it ought to be a space infused by the kind of imaginative awareness that enables those involved to imagine alternative possibilities for their own becoming and their group's becoming.[20]

SUMMARY: LESSONS LEARNED

This chapter begins and ends with a quotation from Maxine Greene that challenges us to build communities of learners that imagine alternatives for what our lives and the lives of the group could become. From this opening quotation, we explored ways to create professional learning communities. These were developed further by examining:

- some ways to create professional learning communities through aesthetic experiences for both teachers and students;
- examples of bonding through professional books to create professional learning communities;
- examples of bonding through award-winning literature;
- ways to build a sense of community through knowledge of our nation's core values.

Following these considerations of professional learning communities, the chapter presents the concept of public pedagogy as specifically seen in the chaos created over CRT. These reactions describe:

- a particular concept of authentic dialogue;
- a strategic-planning process;
- specific ways to develop a school district's mission and embodiment of it in a mission statement;
- several strategies for transformational educational leaders to build bridges so as to communicate effectively to several different constituencies across the school district.

NOTES

1. Maxine Greene, *Releasing the Imagination* (San Francisco: Jossey-Bass, 1995), 39.
2. Ibid.
3. H. G. Bissinger, *Friday Night Lights* (New York: Harper Perennial, 1991).
4. John Dewey, *The School and Society, The Child and the Curriculum* (Chicago: The University of Chicago Press, 1900, 1990).
5. Raymond Callahan, *Education and the Cult of Efficiency* (Chicago: The University of Chicago Press, 1962).
6. Stephen Jay Gould, *The Mismeasure of Man* (New York: W.W. Norton and Company, 1981).
7. Grant Wiggins, *Assessing Student Performance* (San Francisco: Jossey-Bass, 1993).

8. Toni Morrison, *The Bluest Eye* (New York: Penguin Group, 1970).

9. Tommy Orange, *There, There* (New York, Vintage Books, 2019).

10. Educator Resources, "American Indian Urban Relocation," *National Archives*, https://www.archives.gov/education/lessons/indian-relocation.html (accessed November 5, 2021).

11. This author first became aware of this in 2004 when a fifth-grade teacher in Philadelphia gave him an email from the building principal that told teachers not to teach social studies from October until April. This allotted time was to be used to concentrate on math instead because the benchmark standardized tests showed a math deficiency. In recent conversations with several educators, this practice appears not to be an anomaly as late as October, 2021.

12. Marlene Lang, "T/E board meeting packed over critical race theory," *Patch*, June 16, 2021, https://patch.com/pennsylvania/te/t-e-school-board-meeting-packed-over-critical-race-theory (accessed June 18, 2021).

13. Joe Heim, Hannah Natanson, and Tom Jackman, "Residents left fuming, fearful after contentious Loudoun County school board meeting," *The Washington Post*, June 23, 2021, https://www.washingtonpost.com/local/education/loudoun-schools-transgender-critical-race-theory/2021/06/23/1691dfc2-d453-11eb-ae54-515e2f63d37d_story.html (accessed November 14, 2021).

14. Ibid.

15. Alexander Sidorkin, *Beyond Discourse: Education, the Self, and Dialogue* (Albany: State University of New York Press, 1999), 4.

16. Ibid., 14.

17. Ibid., 18.

18. William J. Cook, *Strategic Planning for American's Schools (Montgomery: Cambridge Management Group and Arlington, American Association of School Adminsitrators, 1990)* (Arlington, Virginia, 1990).

19. Owen J. Roberts School District Mission Statement, adopted April 8, 1991.

20. Ibid., Greene, *Releasing the Imagination*.

About the Author

Terrance L. Furin was a social studies teacher for twelve years in Parma, Ohio. He was also a public school superintendent for twenty-two years—eleven in Ohio and eleven in Pennsylvania. He is currently an affiliate professor at Saint Joseph's University in Philadelphia, where he teaches in the educational leadership department's doctoral program helping to prepare transformational leaders. He resides with his wife, Mary Ann, in Saint Peters, Pennsylvania.

www.ingramcontent.com/pod-product-compliance
Lightning Source LLC
Chambersburg PA
CBHW020739230426
43665CB00009B/492